D0199674

The JOurneY Between Us

*My Faith Walk: Overcoming Grief
to Finding JOY in the JOurneY*

Lisa McGrath

WESTBOW
PRESS®
A DIVISION OF THOMAS NELSON
& ZONDERVAN

WestBow Press books may be ordered through booksellers or by contacting:

WestBow Press
A Division of Thomas Nelson & Zondervan
1663 Liberty Drive
Bloomington, IN 47403
www.westbowpress.com
1 (866) 928-1240

ISBN: 978-1-9736-3996-1 (sc)
ISBN: 978-1-9736-3998-5 (hc)
ISBN: 978-1-9736-3997-8 (e)

Library of Congress Control Number: 2018910982

Print information available on the last page.

WestBow Press rev. date: 9/27/2018

This book is dedicated with love and
gratitude to my amazing family:

My wonderful husband Scott and the Fab Five:
Benton, Jaren, Lilian, Lynsi, and Layci as well as our
Jennison, McGrath, Kanak, and Winebrenner families.
It is also dedicated in honor and memory of
Jason Kanak 6/7/1977–7/30/2008
and
Cari McGrath 11/19/1978–8/29/2008
as we remember them on their tenth Angel Anniversary.

Contents

Chapter 1

This Is God's Story; I'm Just Writing It

How does one even begin to write a book about one's life? What would even make someone *want* to write a book about oneself? I mean, couldn't that be construed as a tad egotistical or conceited? Do people who write books about themselves just all of a sudden one day say, "I am such an amazing, important person that I should really write a book about myself"? Then again, aren't we all amazing, important people? Of course we are, especially in the eyes of God— and probably our mothers. Not every amazing, important person in this world will write a book about himself or herself. Maybe writing is not his or her thing. It's really not my thing either. It's not that I can't do it. It is just that I tend to get a little wordy and off subject and try to incorporate my sense of humor, which not everyone gets. And I probably do not follow all the rules of grammar and all that stuff I learned a long time ago in school. Plus I am a pretty busy person.

This may be jumping ahead a little in my story, but I have five kids, a husband, a part-time job, a big house to take care of, soccer, wrestling, football, cross country, volleyball, dance, boy scouts, girl scouts, piano lessons, music concerts, bunco, the gym, grocery shopping, mom-busing, salon appointments, etc. Aside from all that, I must factor in time for text messages, emails, Facebook, eBay, Zulily, and other online shopping because I *need* to know what is going on in the world. And my kids need clothes. And I maybe, sort of, kind of have an addiction. But that is irrelevant. *Anyhoo,* my point is that I am fairly busy with the daunting day-to-day tasks of just being me. But hey, I think I will write a book because I am an amazing, important person. At least that is what I am told by my mother.

Even though I am writing this story, it's not really *my* story; it is God's story. I am just placing the events that God has led me through into words. It's easy to give Him the glory and praise for everything wonderful that has happened in my life, but what about the rough times? What about the tragedy? Well, I still give God the glory because if it were not for my faith, I might have never made it through the rough times. I am sure you have heard multiple versions of the saying "God only gives you what you can handle." I don't believe this. One reason I do not believe it is because it's not from scripture. I also do not believe that God *gives us* our circumstances. I don't believe that He makes things happen to us or allows things to happen to us. What I believe, and what scripture supports in multiple references, is that He promises never to leave us or forsake us, and He will always be with us to help us handle what we've been given.

Chapter 2

In the Beginning ...

It makes sense to start with a little bit about my background.

I grew up in Healy, a very small town in western Kansas. I was born a Christian. What does that actually mean? No, it doesn't mean that when I was born, the doctor held me up to my parents and announced, "It's a girl, and she's a Christian!" But wouldn't that be convenient? To me, it means my parents were Christians, and we regularly attended and were very active in the Methodist church in Healy. I was baptized, was confirmed, and grew up attending church there. I went to Sunday school, Bible school, and youth group, and I even played the piano and organ for church service all through high school. I grew up learning about God, Jesus, the Bible, and prayer and automatically considered myself a Christian because that was what I was taught.

My Christian foundation was laid by my parents, other family members, and my church family. Although I didn't love getting up for church every Sunday morning, it was expected, and it was our routine. Although not regularly at first, I even felt compelled to go to church during college because it just made me feel better about myself and my life.

So I don't have a specific moment or time or event that led me to accept Jesus as my Savior, and for a while, I felt odd about that. As I got older, when I heard people share their testimonies about how they became Christians, I didn't think my testimony was anything phenomenal. But friends, over the years I have learned that is far from the truth. Your testimony isn't just about how you became a Christian and accepted Jesus Christ as your Savior. It is also about sharing the ways that God has molded you and shaped you as a Christian and your personal witness and account of the unending love that He has shown you and how it has deepened your spiritual walk and beliefs.

I loved being from a small town and attending a small school. I didn't always love living a whole four miles out in the country because I often missed hanging out with friends, but country life did have its perks. It's funny to me that as a kid I thought four miles out of town was excruciating. Now, as an adult living in the city, it's ten miles from our house to the high school my kids attend. I never had more than ten kids in my class, and that was my graduating senior class, which had a foreign exchange student and a transfer from a neighboring town. So the core of my class from K to 12 hovered right around eight classmates. Yep, eight kids.

It's hard for my kids to imagine, seeing as how they have hundreds of kids in their classes. I sometimes wish my kids could experience small-school and small-town life, but they are perfectly happy where we are. They don't know any different. One major perk of going to a small-town school was that I always made the team, no matter what the sport. In fact, it wasn't uncommon to have to recruit kids to go out for sports just so we could have a team. As far as girls' sports were concerned, we had only volleyball, basketball, and track, and I loved all three. My high school sports career definitely made for a lot of wonderful memories—some of the best of my life. We were never state champions in any team sports, but we sure had some great seasons and a lot of fun. I was, however, a state champion in discus my junior year, which was a wonderful experience and a highlight of high school.

Playing sports was a big part of high school for me, but academics as well as music, drama, quiz bowl, student council, and homecoming queen made for a very well-rounded high school experience. I had multiple offers from colleges to play volleyball and basketball, but by the end of my senior year, I had determined that I was a bit burned out on sports and wanted to focus on my education. I had researched many careers my junior and senior years and knew that I wanted to do something in the medical field. I had received multiple scholarship offers from Fort Hays State and was intrigued by their radiology program. After visiting the school, as well as a few hospitals to tour their radiology departments, I knew that it was a career I would like to pursue. I was told that it was an intense program, but based on my grades and test scores, I could definitely be considered a candidate for the program even though it was uncommon for incoming freshmen to be accepted. First, I had to apply to the program and be selected for an interview.

A few weeks after I sent my application, I received a letter stating that I had been selected for an interview. I was excited but quite nervous. The interview would be conducted by a panel of about fifteen people. At first, I thought I would be intimidated, but for some reason, my attitude was that I had nothing to lose. I was going to attend Fort Hays regardless of whether I was accepted into the program, so if I didn't get accepted as a freshman, I would just take whatever classes administrators recommended and apply again.

They must have liked me because I was indeed accepted into the program. I would graduate high school in May and start college in June. It was scary yet exciting!

So in June 1996, off I went to Fort Hays State University in Hays, Kansas. I can honestly say that I had a blast in college. I was pretty straitlaced and not much of a partier in high school, so I definitely came out of my shell once I got to college. I wasn't a wild child and didn't get in any trouble, but I made a lot of wonderful friends, was involved on campus and in intramural sports, and did attend my fair share of parties. The radiology program did prove to be intense, so I had to be dedicated to studying and staying on track with my classes. High school came easily to me, and I didn't have to study much at all, so this program was a good challenge.

Just three short years later, in 1999, I received my bachelor's degree in medical diagnostic imaging. That is a fancy degree name for radiologic technologist, which is a fancy name for someone who takes x-rays. And again, I said *technologist,* not technician. That word drives me crazy (along with every other college-educated radiologic technologist). I started my career at Hays Medical Center, worked a variety of shifts, and gained a lot of valuable experience.

In November of 1999, I met the man who would become my husband. I met him at a bar, and he was wearing pajamas—Denver Broncos pajamas specifically. The bar was called The Home Party Club, and thankfully it was pajama night, so this wasn't his normal going-out attire. My mom had always said I should go to church to meet a man, but apparently the bar has more options. It's probably also not appropriate to wear your pajamas to church, not that it is totally appropriate to wear them to a bar either. Walmart is totally fine and socially accepted. But his Denver Broncos pajamas, as well as the fact that he was clearly confident enough to wear them to the bar, definitely caught my attention. The man's name was Jason, and he was an accounting major working on his master's degree. He was also on the Fort Hays State golf team.

What a great guy, almost too good to be true. I had not had the best luck with dating and relationships. I was pretty good at a lot of things, but dating was not one of them. In a high school the size of mine, you were either best friends with most of the guys or else related to them, so dating wasn't an option. I did date a guy from another town in high school, but once I went to college, I knew I didn't want to be tied down. I needed to be free to be me. I went on a few dates during college but nothing serious until Jason. It didn't take long to know he was "the one."

We were married November 17, 2001, and started our perfect little life together. I continued to work at the hospital, and Jason worked for an accounting firm in Hays.

In the summer of 2002 we found out we were expecting. Unfortunately, the pregnancy ended in a miscarriage at five weeks, and I was devastated. To date, this was the most difficult situation I had experienced. I found myself questioning *what if we would not be able to have kids*? I finally just had to remind myself that this was not in my hands. It was in God's hand. All I could do was pray about it and have hope that some day we would indeed experience the joy of a child. Seven months later, I became pregnant again, and although I felt nervous, I was very excited and relieved.

We were blessed with our first child, a son, Jaren, in February of 2004. A little over a year later my mom happened to mention to me that one of the x-ray techs at the hospital in Scott City was leaving. The imaging director had approached my mom and asked if she thought I would be interested. She said she told them that I probably wouldn't be interested, since we liked living in Hays. At first, I didn't give it much consideration, but the more I thought about how important family was to me, especially now that we had a child, I decided that it might be a great opportunity. So, despite us both having jobs that we really loved, we made the decision to move closer to my family and start a new chapter of our lives.

Chapter 3

Moving Back Home

In the summer of 2005 we moved to Scott City. I took the job at the Scott County Hospital as the chief technologist of the radiology department. I had a lot more responsibility but also had the opportunity to broaden my skills in some new areas. I was excited that I would be working with one of my best friends and a department full of wonderful people.

At the time of our relocation, there were no accounting jobs available for Jason in Scott City, so he found a job at a firm in Garden City. This job would require a forty-minute commute, one way. Neither one of us really liked that he would have to commute, but it would be a good career opportunity for him, so he accepted it. He did really enjoy working there and did gain very valuable experience. Tax season was exceptionally brutal with extra hours both early in the morning and late at night, plus having the windshield time added in. I soon understood why accountant spouses are often called "tax widows/widowers" from January through April, and also why April 15 is a holiday in the accounting world. I honestly do not know how he did it, but he never complained.

We were both excited when he was contacted about a job opportunity in Scott City. He went to work at a small individually owned accounting firm. He absolutely *loved* the job, and the icing on the cake was that his boss loved golf as much as Jason did, so you can imagine where they spent a lot of time. I then learned what a "golf widow" was from April 15 through—well, as long as the weather cooperated and the courses were open.

We felt truly at home in Scott City and that it was where we were meant to be. We had become very involved in the Methodist church there. We attended Sunday school and church regularly. I had joined a new women's Bible study group and convinced Jason to join the men's study group. Those groups became a big part of our lives and really helped us both grow in our faith. Jason was never really very open about his faith; more of a "quiet Christian" I liked to call him. So you can imagine my surprise when on our way home from study one Wednesday night, he looked at me and said, "I want to thank you for convincing me to join men's Bible study." He proceeded to tell me how much he enjoyed the group, and if it were not for me in his life, he would not have grown so much in his faith. Looking back now, that was an important proclamation, which left no doubt in my mind that he had accepted the Lord as his Savior.

The summer of 2008, a new pastor took the pulpit at the church. Pastor Dennis was a wonderful pastor with a very interesting background. He had not been a pastor all that long. If I remember right, he had worked for a co-op in a small town before he felt called to ministry. He and his wife were each other's second marriage. Despite their fifteen-year age difference (she was older), they fell in love and eventually married.

Once Pastor Dennis got somewhat settled in the church, he decided that he wanted to visit each of the Sunday school classes to get to know people. Ironically (you will soon see why), the Sunday he visited our class, we were sharing our personal testimonies. Jason and I both gave our testimonies that Sunday morning in the presence of our new pastor. Again, Jason credited me with being a big influence on his faith walk, which was a very nice compliment. And once again, it was verbalized that he not only believed in God but had accepted him as his Lord and Savior.

Not long after moving and feeling settled, we decided we were ready to add to our family. Our very first pregnancy back in 2002 ended in a miscarriage, and then it took another seven months before I became pregnant with Jaren. Although it was a bit discouraging, we did not consider that time frame to be anything out of the ordinary. Unfortunately, though, we spent the next two and a half years trying to conceive with no success. Talk about discouraging. Up to that point, I had never really struggled with anything as much as I struggled then with infertility.

Over the course of those two years, I prayed and prayed. My family prayed, my friends prayed, and my women's Bible study prayed. I admit I was a little frustrated with God at this point and was having a hard time understanding why we were not having any luck. It seemed as if everywhere I went there were pregnant women. We loved being parents and we so badly wanted Jaren to have a sibling.

We finally decided to try fertility treatments and after the second month it worked! I found out in late December of 2007 that I was finally pregnant. At that time Jaren was really into Superman, so I made an iron-on transfer with the superman symbol on it with the words, "I am going to be a 'Super' big brother." I put the shirt on him so that he was wearing it to surprise Jason when he came home that day. Our prayers had been answered; we were finally going to have another child.

This pregnancy was totally different from my pregnancy with Jaren, so I figured it had to be a girl. Aside from that, from the very first time we told Jaren that Mommy was going to have a baby, he said, "I am going to have a little sister." I am not going to lie, I was hoping for a girl. If only I had known then what I know now about little girls ... just kidding. Anyway, it was eventually confirmed by sonogram that we were having a little girl. *Yay!* Let the uncontrollable shopping begin! I decided to decorate her room in brown and pink, so one weekend, after tax season was over and there was no golf tournament, we painted her room. We were getting really excited. I had this feeling she was going to be a "Daddy's girl."

Some close family friends from my home town wanted to host a baby shower for me since it was a little girl. It was set for Wednesday evening, July 30, 2008, in Healy, which is twenty-four miles from Scott City. Wednesdays were also men's night at the golf course, but Jason didn't really want me driving over to Healy by myself with Jaren, so he offered to go along. I remember calling him at work on Wednesday morning to remind him about the shower, and I even reiterated that I could go by myself if he wanted to play golf. But he said it was no big deal to miss golf and that he was planning to go. He and my dad were planning to take Jaren to the swimming pool while Mom and I went to the shower.

The shower was wonderful. It was so much fun to get all the "girlie" stuff and to see all the ladies and girls there. One of the best presents was from my mom. It was a variety of items that were mine when I was a baby. It was very sentimental. I was pretty worn out, though, after working all day, so I decided it was time to go meet the boys and head back home. They were still at the swimming pool, and Jaren, of course, did not want to get out. Once we finally got him out of the pool and everyone dressed, we loaded up to head back home. As my mom gave us our goodbye hugs, I remember her saying, "Drive safe and watch out for deer." As we always did, we said we would.

Chapter 4

Jesus, Take the Wheel

Jason always did the driving. I *hate* to drive. I don't know why, I just do. It almost pained me to drive to work every day. There were days I would even ask Jason to drive me to the grocery store. I know, I was spoiled. I have gotten better, but still, if given the choice, I will definitely ride rather than drive.

I don't really much care to ride either. I am not the world's greatest traveler by any stretch of the imagination. I have traveler's attention deficit disorder (TADD), I am sure of it. (And no, it's not a real thing.) I have attention span issues in a lot of other areas too, but those are different chapters, maybe even other books. I like to go places; I just like to be there fast.

I had never hit a deer, but I had heard many stories of people who had. I had also seen plenty of deer dead on the side of the road. Still, I hadn't ever heard of anyone actually being killed in a deer-related accident. I remember the time my mom hit one on her way to work. She was less than a mile away from the road we lived on, and one jumped out of the ditch and hit her. It shattered her windshield and dented the front, totaling the car, but thankfully she was not hurt, just extremely shook up. They can sure do major damage.

Riding in a vehicle at eight months pregnant was brutal for me. My pregnant body did not like to bend into a normal sitting position, so it was very uncomfortable to sit in a vehicle. I remember thinking how uncomfortable I was that evening and wishing we would hurry up and get home. The last time I remember looking at the clock, I think it read 9:26. It was just starting to get dark enough that headlights were necessary. I cannot even tell you whether Jason and I were having a conversation. If I had to guess, I would say that we were probably talking about the shower and maybe some of the gifts we received or maybe even how our days were. I don't know really. I don't remember that.

What I do remember is that I had closed my eyes for a moment, and then I heard Jason say something. It could have been "Oh, my"; it could have been "Oh no"; it could have been anything, I don't remember that either. All I know is it got my attention, and I opened my eyes. At first all I saw were the headlights of another car on the other side of the road. Pretty typical, I thought. But then I saw what he saw. There was a deer just standing there on the other side of the highway. Just standing there.

The next thing I was aware of was a huge crashing noise. I remember putting my head down and my arms over my head. It all happened so fast that I wasn't even sure what *had* happened. When the crashing noise subsided, I looked up to try and process it all. First of all, I assumed that we were stopped. Then I assumed that we were all OK, just very freaked out by what had just happened.

The first thing I realized was that I was covered in shattered glass. I turned to look at Jason, and what I saw will be embedded in my brain forever. He was unconscious. His head was tilted back against the headrest, and his arms were limp at his sides. I started screaming his name, but there was no response.

I was so focused on Jason that I really don't know how long it took me to realize that we were still moving. I grabbed the wheel in a frantic attempt to keep us on the highway. I was afraid if we hit the ditch or a culvert, we would roll. Now how in the world was I going to get this truck stopped? There was no way I could crawl into the driver's seat or reach the brake with my foot. My next thought was to try and get the gearshift out of drive. I was able to, but that still didn't stop us.

I have no idea how far we actually traveled. What seemed like forever all happened in about two minutes. Mind you, I had an eight-month-pregnant belly, and I was leaning over a console trying to steer a runaway truck while my husband was unconscious in the driver's seat. I needed help from the Lord. All I could do was pray that He would give me the strength to stop this truck and save my family.

It finally came to me that the only way I was going to get us stopped was to reach down and hit the brake with my hand. I tried to reach down with my left hand, keeping my right hand on the wheel and trying to maintain a line of sight out the window. No luck, as I couldn't reach the pedal doing that. Finally, I just slid headfirst over the console until I could reach the brake and slammed on it as hard as I could with my hand. It worked, thank God!

I didn't know where we stopped, whether we were on the road, on the shoulder, or in the ditch; I did not care. The main things on my mind were Jason and calling for help. And then suddenly the realization hit me that I had not heard a peep out of Jaren. *Oh my goodness— Jaren!* As I yelled his name, I turned around to the backseat and was relieved to see his frightened little eyes staring back at me. "Mommy, I am all right. What's wrong with Daddy?" *Again*, thank God he was OK.

I fumbled around for my purse and my cell phone; luckily it was within reach. I grabbed my phone, praying that I had service. With only one bar of reception, I frantically dialed 911 and to my relief was connected. I can't remember exactly what I said, but I do remember the dispatch lady saying, "Ma'am, you need to calm down." *Seriously?* Then the call dropped. I called back again, trying to be calmer, but fortunately she had gotten enough information from me the first time and told me that help was on the way.

I then called the hospital and told them that Jason was unconscious and badly hurt. I told them he had a serious head injury and that he would probably need to be flown out right away. Being "on call" after routine business hours was a responsibility of my job, so I was fully aware that sometimes it takes a while in a rural facility for the doctor or whoever is on call to get to the hospital after the patient has arrived. I knew they needed to be there when Jason arrived, so I thought I had better call ahead. Sometimes when you are in the medical profession, you know too much, and that can be good and bad.

Chapter 5

Please, God, Answer My Prayer, and Make It Quick

I had checked Jason for a pulse, and he still had one. He was breathing, which was also encouraging. I was fearful that he had a serious head injury. I kept saying his name in hopes of some conscious response. Jaren was screaming "Daddy, wake up!" Poor little boy, he was only four years old and had no idea what was going on. He kept asking "Why won't Daddy wake up?" I was concerned that Jason also had a neck injury, so I did my best to keep his neck and head supported.

It seemed to be taking forever for emergency personnel to respond. I was relieved when I finally saw headlights, but then they passed. Believe it or not, a couple more vehicles passed by. You would think a truck stopped in the middle of the road would be a concern for some, but I guess not. "Ma'am, you need to calm down" kept playing over and over in my head, and I realized maybe she was right. At that moment, the only thing that I could do to calm my nerves was pray. I held Jason's head in my hands, and I prayed. I prayed that he would be OK. I prayed that help would come soon, as I knew time was not on our side at this point.

Finally, I could see flashing lights. It was a police officer. I honestly think he had no idea what to think or say when he approached our vehicle and saw us. He knew who we were. His wife used to be the secretary at Jason's office. He was very calm and encouraging, especially as he tried to calm Jaren, who was still in the backseat screaming for his daddy to wake up.

A few minutes later the ambulance and an entourage of EMTs arrived. I was so fixated on Jason and what they were doing with him that I was totally ignoring the people trying to get me and Jaren out of the truck. The EMTs worked very quickly. It didn't take them long to get Jason out of the truck and into the ambulance. Someone had managed to coax me out of the truck, so I was just standing in the middle of the road with Jaren clinging to my leg watching them load him up. I know there were people all around me trying to talk to me, but I didn't hear any of them.

Suddenly Jaren yelled,, "Mommy, what is wrong with your stomach?" The first thing I thought was *Oh no, he has a head injury and forgot that I am pregnant.* A wave of panic rushed over me, but then I looked down at my stomach and realized that I was a mess from the accident. I honestly hadn't even paid any attention to myself. I didn't know if I was even hurt. It didn't matter. It was then that I noticed that Jaren was also a mess and covered in pieces of glass. Regardless, I grabbed him up and hugged him tight. I told him I was OK, and everything was going to be all right. He just kept saying he was scared and asking about Daddy.

The ambulance was ready to take off and head to town. One of the EMTs and a highway patrolman then approached me and said that we would follow the ambulance in the EMT's vehicle. For some reason, it dawned on me that we had just come from the baby shower, and all those gifts were in the back of the truck. I remember telling the highway patrolman that I knew it seemed insignificant, but if they could retrieve all those gifts for me, I would really appreciate it.

The ride into town seemed to take forever. The accident occurred about four miles east of the junction of Highway 83 and Highway 4, so we were about twelve miles from Scott City. I held Jaren on my lap in the front seat of the EMT's pickup. I know it's gross, but all I could smell was deer feces in Jaren's hair. I felt so sorry for him, as he just kept crying and asking about his daddy. I will never forget the EMT telling him, "Your daddy is going to be fine." I don't hold that against him because I know he was only trying to help console a very scared and upset little boy, but it was definitely false hope for me.

As we approached town, I was amazed to see that law enforcement had set up a barricade which allowed for easy access straight to the hospital. Once we pulled up to the emergency room doors, they had already arrived with Jason and had taken him inside. I was thankful that they had been ready and waiting. As Jaren and I walked in the door, they quickly took us to the ER room across the hall from where they had taken Jason and began assessing us. All I wanted to do, though, was see Jason and find out how he was doing.

It was hard for them to accurately assess Jaren and me for injuries because our clothes and skin were very soiled. A nurse practitioner and nurse took Jaren to shower him off so that they could get a better look at him. The nurses immediately hooked me up to the pregnancy monitor to check the baby. Even though he wasn't on call, a second doctor had also come in so that one doctor could be with Jason and one with me. I was absolutely amazed and humbled by all the staff. I felt blessed and proud to call them my coworkers. I cannot even imagine what it was like for all of them though, to see people they knew come in looking the way we did. I kept asking about Jason, and everyone just kept saying, "Dr. Cupp is working on him."

The next thing I remember is my coworker from the radiology department, who was on call, coming into the room. She hugged me right away and then grabbed some wet rags and started helping clean me up. I remember thinking, *Why is she in here and not doing Jason's CT scans?* I knew he had a head injury and would need a CT (CAT) scan. I looked at her and asked if she knew how he was. Huge tears welled in her eyes, and all she said was, "You know," as she grabbed me and hugged me tight. It took a few seconds for her words to register.

Dr. Cupp then came in the room and informed me that Jason had gone into cardiac arrest on the way to the hospital. He had given him a lot of drugs to try and revive him, and he was going to keep working, but it didn't look good. Whoa, wait a second. *What did he just say?* I honestly did not expect any of this. I was sure that because of Jason's head injury, we would be on our way to a neurosurgeon in Wichita. I *never* expected that he wouldn't make it. This *could not* be happening.

I was holding it together fairly well considering the circumstances. It's called shock and disbelief. However, once my parents arrived, I broke down and lost control of my emotions. After the accident occurred and I had called 911 and the hospital, the next call I made or tried to make was to my parents. Their line was busy, which meant the phone was off the hook because they had call waiting. I tried to call sixteen times, and then I finally called my uncle, who lived a few miles from my parents. I told him that their phone was busy and asked if he could please give them the message that we had been in an accident. He apparently got ahold of them, because they arrived at the hospital not long after we did.

Both my mom and dad came into the room with tears streaming down their faces. My mom grabbed me right away, and I burst into tears. All I could say between sobbing and gasping for air was "I can't do this," over and over again. "I can't have a baby without him" was another thought I expressed. She just held me tight while I cried and cried. My mom is and will always be my rock. She has always known what to say to comfort or encourage me in any situation I present her with. But right then, in that situation, my mom did not know what to say. She just cried with me.

Chapter 6

Really, God, Why?

Dr. Cupp is an amazing person and wonderful doctor. He was also our neighbor, which I am sure made it all the more difficult for him. Living and practicing medicine in a small town has got to be tough sometimes, especially when tragic events like this one strike. I can only imagine what it was like for him to have to come back across that hall and tell his patient, his neighbor, that there was nothing more he could do. Not only had he lost a patient, he had lost a friend and neighbor who was also a father and husband. He then had to think about caring for me as his patient, eight months pregnant and suddenly widowed, and eventually deliver what would be a fatherless baby girl. I will always admire that man for his strength and courage, not to mention his professionalism.

After he delivered the devastating news, he told us that we could see Jason and say our goodbyes. Goodbyes? What an unfathomable concept at the time. No warning, no time, no "heads-up." This was not exactly what I had in mind for the day when I woke up that morning. This was just all so incomprehensible.

I was numb; in shock; in a dream … no nightmare. Someone *please wake me up*! But it was really happening. My parents, one on each side, helped me into a wheelchair and wheeled me across the hall. There he lay. The first thing I noticed was his left hand as his arm lay lifeless off the side of the bed. I saw his wedding ring. *This is my husband* … was *my husband. How could this have happened; how can it be happening?*

They wheeled me closer, and I stood to see him. I honestly don't think any words even came out of my mouth because just as quickly as I stood, my parents had to catch me as I collapsed out of overwhelming grief and shock. All I could do was cry. As much as I regret it now, I could not be in this room. I pleaded for them to get me out. I had no strength. I felt lifeless.

All I could do was question God: *Why? What is this plan? It makes absolutely no sense.* The accident itself was a freak, one-of-a-kind incident. Why did it happen? As far as I was concerned, there was nothing going on around me. I had slipped into another realm of being. Nothing made sense, and I was too broken to even try and make sense of it. I guess maybe I was one of those "nothing like this is ever going to happen to me" people. Well, it happened. I just hadn't accepted it yet and had not a clue how to even begin to try.

The last place I wanted to be was at the hospital, the place where my husband was pronounced dead. The doctors insisted I stay the night for observation and to be on the fetal monitor to check the baby as well. The last thing I wanted to do was see anyone or talk to anyone. I have no idea how they all had heard, but word had definitely traveled fast as family members and friends started to arrive. Looking back, I am very thankful that they were all there and that they cared as much as they did for me and my family.

I was especially thankful for Jason's boss, Rohn, and his wife, Traci, and everything they did that devastating night. I think one of the

EMTs had called Rohn, and he and Traci were there immediately, helping in any way they could. It was Rohn who made that dreaded call to Jason's parents. As a parent, that has to be the worst call you could ever get, especially since they lived in Atwood, almost two hours away.

At this point, I knew that I needed to turn my focus to Jaren. The nurses had gotten him cleaned up and had checked him over. Thankfully, he was fine physically, with just a few minor cuts and scrapes. But what about emotionally? I didn't know how to tell him or explain any of this to him. I had no idea if he would understand or how he would react. I wasn't even sure I had the strength or the words to even talk to him and tell him what had happened. It made me sick that he'd had to witness what he did. I prayed that he would not be scarred or have nightmares from it. They had already taken him to the hospital room I was going to occupy for the night, and Traci was there with him. She had bundled him up and was holding him tight, rocking him.

Chapter 7

The Accident Report—How It Happened. But Still: Why?

There is truly no way to describe how I smelled. I work in the medical field; I grew up with brothers and a feedlot in my backyard. Still, this was by far the worst smell I had ever encountered. I desperately needed a shower, but I didn't know if I had the strength to stand as long as it would take to get this smell to go away. It had to be done, though.

I remember reaching up to wash my matted hair and feeling the tiny shards of glass all over my head. I just stood there in the shower with the warm water running over me, crying and wishing that the water would wash my pain away. This was the first time I had been alone since arriving at the hospital, so it gave me some time to try and wrap my head around what was happening here. It still just felt like a dream, or rather, a nightmare.

I tried to recall the events of the night. It was just all so unbelievable, but I was there, and I knew it had happened. Even still, I could not believe it. *Why did this happen to us? Why, God? What had we done to deserve this? Why Jason? Why? Why? Why?* The questions just kept popping into my head, and I could not understand. We were going to be having a baby in a month—a baby that it took us two and a half years to conceive. And now this baby was going to come into this world without a father. This was just not possible. It had to be a dream, and I just needed to wake up.

The sound of a voice calling my name and asking if I was doing all right snapped me back to reality. My nurse was outside waiting for me to finish so that she could help me get settled into my bed and hooked up to the fetal monitor. I didn't like it, but I understood the reason for it. At this point, I really did want to make sure everything was OK with my baby girl. I will, however, never understand why hospital beds have to be so uncomfortable. Aren't patients in hospitals usually there to feel better or recuperate? They are not made with tall people in mind either. I am five-eleven by the way and do not fit well in a hospital bed. I suppose the bed was the least of my problems, but it definitely did not help matters much.

Not long after the nurses (who subsequently all had tears streaming down their faces as they cared for me) got me settled, a highway patrolman arrived and wanted to talk to me. As I previously mentioned, I wasn't really in the mood to talk to anyone but I figured I should probably make an exception for law enforcement. I do admire the way law enforcement handle themselves in situations like these. They witness the most horrific situations that anyone could ever be in, and yet they go right on doing their jobs with thorough professionalism. I observed this same characteristic of EMTs, doctors, nurses, and everyone else at the hospital who was part of this horrible tragedy.

Officer Bradley came into my room and sat down beside my bed. He started out by giving his condolences. Then he said that after assessing what they could in the dark, he wanted to commend me for my actions and my quick thinking, which resulted in getting the vehicle stopped. He stated that it was unexplainable, but after seeing the skid marks from the truck, he knew that had we traveled a few more feet, we would have hit a culvert, and most likely the vehicle would have rolled.

He was the one to first fill me in on details as to what appeared to have happened. He told me that an elderly couple in a Prius was eastbound on Highway 4 when a deer suddenly appeared in their lane. They then hit the deer, stopped their car as soon as they could, and called 911. Their car was undrivable at this point, so they had to wait for law enforcement to arrive to assess the situation. They had no idea that the deer had then flown through the window of our vehicle in the westbound lane. Another highway patrol officer had responded to their accident, so the two patrolmen worked together to piece together the puzzle of the accident.

According to the accident report, after we hit the deer, the truck traveled 214 feet 8 inches west before going into the north ditch. It then traveled 296 feet 10 inches in the ditch before I was able to steer it back up onto the highway. Once I was finally able to stop the truck, we had traveled half a mile from the point of impact. It was surprising to me that they could come up with such detailed measurements. The accident report also said that I told him that I was unable to reach the brake but was able to put the vehicle into park to make it stop moving. I *wish* it had stopped moving after I did that, but it didn't. That extra fifteen hundred or so feet was due to me trying to figure out how I *was* going to get it to stop moving. At the time, it meant absolutely nothing and just angered me because the outcome was still that my husband was killed. That was all I could focus on. I didn't feel like a hero or anyone to be commended because I couldn't save my husband. But in reality, I did save my babies and myself. Granted, I will admit there were times I wished I hadn't survived, but those thoughts were only out of deep pain and grief.

The situation itself caused a major faith struggle for me for quite a while. When people would tell me they didn't know how I did it, I would say that I felt as if the Lord had taken the wheel and helped guide me in getting the vehicle stopped. But then on the other hand, He took my husband. As I said, that was a major source of conflict for me. I didn't understand how our Lord could help me do what I did to save myself and my children but at the same time take my husband and their father.

Chapter 8

Facing Family and Friends

I don't know exactly how many friends and family members had congregated outside in the halls at this point, but I still did not want to see any of them. I am not one who likes a lot of attention put on me, so I just didn't want to face all these people who were focused on me and felt sorry for me. I was probably being a little selfish, but at the time, I didn't know what to think or do. Every time someone new would show up, my mom would come and ask if I wanted to see them, to which I would say no.

However, the time she came in and said, "Heather and Kate are here," I burst into tears and agreed to see them. They were two of my coworkers and closest friends in Scott City. Kate and I were practically neighbors as well, and our neighborhood spent a lot of time together. They both ran in crying too and hugged me at the same time. I know that was hard for them, and I know they had no idea what to say, but the mere fact that they came to be there for me meant more than words. I truly felt the same way about everyone who gathered there that evening, but I guess I just needed to see two of my closest friends the most.

Bless Kate's heart, she had just gone through a heartbreaking second-trimester miscarriage and had been on leave from work with no definite plans as to when she would return. We had told her to take all the time she needed for both her physical and emotional well-being. And now she had lost a good friend as well, and she was telling me that she would be back at work the next day and not to worry about work at all. My coworkers were amazing and went above and beyond all expectations to cover for me and run the department in my absence. Work was one of the last things on my mind, but nevertheless it was nice to know that I wouldn't have to worry about it.

With Jason's parents living two hours away in Atwood, I just could not imagine what they were going through after getting that call and then having to travel that two hours to get here. Luckily Joe's (Jason's dad's) sister and her husband drove them. I was terrified to face them. Although I did not know what to say, once they arrived, there really wasn't much to be said. Of course, we all hugged and cried, but their main concern at this point was making sure that Jaren, the baby, and I were all right. The staff had taken Jason's body to one of the empty hospital rooms down the hall so that his parents could see him when they got there. What a nightmare for them as well, to lose a child, their only son. They were a very close-knit family. Jason and Joe had spent a lot of time together in the summer playing golf, and Jason spoke to both his parents on the phone frequently. At the time, Jason's sister, Linda, was living in Louisville, Kentucky, and was also eight-months pregnant. As each other's only sibling, they were very close as well. How horrible for her to be so far away and find out that her big brother had passed away in such a tragic way.

As that night passed, it seemed as if the magnitude of the situation just continued to worsen. Maybe it was the shock wearing off and the realization that it was really happening. Joe spent a very long time in the room with Jason's body. He has always said that he is glad he was able to do that. After we all said our teary goodbyes that night,

Joe, his sister, and his brother-in-law went back to Atwood while Jason's mom, Lynette, stayed in Scott City to be there to help in any way she could. My mom stayed at the hospital with Jaren and me while my dad went back home to Healy. Lynette went to stay at our house—which was a mess, I might add—and as she could not sleep, she spent most of the night cleaning the place. She figured we would probably be having some visitors over the next few days.

I already mentioned how much I loathe hospital beds, but that night was one of the most uncomfortable nights of my life. I was miserable emotionally and physically. With the fetal monitor in place, I had to stay on my back and just could not get comfortable. The nurses had told me that the doctor said they could give me medication if I needed it to relax and sleep. I finally decided that I needed it. I called the nurse, and she came right away to give me the medication. I could see how much it pained my nurses to come in my room. Each nurse would leave the room with tears streaming down her face. They all showed great compassion. Of course, they all knew me fairly well since we often worked together, so I knew they felt sorry for me as well. I don't think I ever did sleep. It would have been nice to go to sleep and wake up and find that it was really all just a dream.

Chapter 9

Planning a Funeral

I would like to say that with the sunrise came hope of a new day. But all it was to me was the first day of being a pregnant, widowed single mom. There was absolutely no hope at this point or none that I could see anyway. I had no idea where to go from here. *Overwhelmed* does not even begin to describe how I was feeling. Of course, I was still pretty numb and still in shock. The doctor came in to check Jaren and me over and determined that we were both physically fine and could be discharged to go home. *To do what?* I wondered. We were going to go home to a house that would never be the same. The man of the house would never step foot in it again. It was still completely unreal. Nevertheless, I did not want to spend another minute in the hospital either, so home we went.

The news of the accident and Jason's death spread through town like wildfire. I think we were home for five minutes when people started calling and coming by. As devastated as I was, I actually felt sorrier for my friends and family, as I knew they had no idea what to say or do. I had no idea what to say or do either. Nevertheless, it did register at once that I had abundant support and was surrounded by so many people who cared and loved me. I really do dislike being the center of attention, so it was a little awkward, to say the least. I am more comfortable being a helper or a consoler than a victim.

I absolutely asked, over and over and over, *"Why me?"* After everything we had been through—trying to get pregnant for over two years and then being overjoyed when we finally succeeded—for the baby's father, my husband, to be killed one month before she was due to be born in a horrific, unimaginable freak accident just did not make any sense, and I did not even know how to feel. Honestly, had it not been for Jaren and my unborn child, I would not have cared whether I lived at this point. Looking back, I had many horrible thoughts, and my emotions really did get the best of me at times. I remember crying and yelling that I didn't even want to have a baby now. It was supposed to be one of the happiest moments of our lives, and now she would have to come into this world without a father. I remember thinking it just wasn't fair.

I honestly don't remember if or how much I prayed in those few days following the accident. The last real memory I have of praying was while we were still sitting in the vehicle after the accident waiting for the ambulance. Fortunately, there were so many people praying for me that I did start to feel the Lord's presence.

Every minute of every day was just hard. But having to see people for the first time and giving or getting that first hug from someone was even beyond hard. Each and every time, I broke down and cried for several minutes. It was actually exhausting. Seeing my and Jason's family members for the first time was probably the most difficult. My middle brother and I had actually not been speaking a whole lot for some reason or another, so seeing him for the first time was very emotional for both of us. Then, seeing Jason's sister was so heartbreaking as well. Jason and Linda were exceptionally close. Aside from that, being pregnant herself made it that much more emotionally overwhelming.

As much as I would have loved to avoid it and not even be involved, there was a funeral to plan. Talk about an overwhelming experience. It was one of those things you never think of having to do at age thirty. I could count on two hands the number of funerals I had even attended, so planning a funeral was far beyond comprehension. At this point, I was in a daze. I was physically conscious and present, but mentally and emotionally I was not anywhere near reality. There is just way too much planning that has to go into a funeral—from casket material, color, size, burial plot, viewing times, funeral times, service details, scriptures, and music, to memorials, flowers, who the pallbearers would be, and what they would wear, etc., etc. Combine that with seven people plus the funeral director working together to agree on arrangements, and you have one very frustrated, exhausted, angry pregnant widow. Everyone kept asking what I thought or what I wanted, and each and every time I would just answer, "I don't care." I just wanted someone to do the planning for me.

It is no secret that I *hate* making decisions in the first place. I am just an easygoing person like that, and I will usually just go along with anything anyone else chooses. So being faced with decisions of this magnitude was way above me. And honestly, I had no idea "what Jason would have wanted," because we never had those conversations. The only thing I knew for sure was that we were going to bury him in a Denver Broncos golf shirt because the Broncos and golf were his two passions, along with his favorite orange cargo shorts. Being an accountant, he had to dress up and wear a tie every single day at work, and he absolutely loathed it, so I knew he would not want to be buried in dressy attire of any kind.

I do have to say that everyone involved worked very well together to assist me with the funeral planning decisions. I wanted it to be respectful and special to honor Jason, but I also just wanted it to be over. The days between when someone dies until the funeral just make you feel like your life is in limbo.

I often say that God has a sense of humor. No, so far none of this is even remotely funny, so let me explain. Jason was an eBay addict. In fact, he had eight eBay auctions going the day he died. He considered himself a bit of a golf club expert and loved to buy and sell golf clubs. Aside from selling, he also did quite a bit of buying, and I often was appalled and, yes, maybe a tad irritated at the "stuff" he would buy. Case in point … one time he bought a beat-up Pepsi can from a "Michael Jackson concert" series. The amount of Denver Broncos memorabilia as well as sports cards he purchased was insane as well.

So back to the humor … the afternoon of the day we planned the funeral we were all sitting around reminiscing at our house when some packages arrived. One of the packages was a size medium baby blue golf polo. Jason was a big guy and wore a size 2XL. There was no way he could have worn it, so I have no idea what that purchase was about. The second package was something I will never forget because it was a typical Jason "impulse buy," as he liked to call them. It was one dozen highlighters. Big deal, right? Well you see, these highlighters were blue with orange caps and the color of the highlighter was orange. I opened them, and no one said a word. We just all busted out in laughter. As I look back on it, we all needed that moment of escape from the devastation and sadness we were all feeling, and a good laugh at Jason's expense came at the perfect time. It was no coincidence to me. God knew. It became very evident to me through this situation that God's timing is always perfect even though some situations are far from perfect.

Chapter 10

Faith like a Child's

Jason passed away July 30, 2008. It was a Wednesday and one I will never forget. The visitation was set for that Friday and the funeral on Saturday. The day he died and the next few days leading up to the funeral were some of the longest, most excruciating days of my life. By the end of each day I wanted to bury myself under my covers and forget everything that had happened. I was drained, physically, mentally, and emotionally. I couldn't eat, I couldn't sleep, and I am pretty sure I was dehydrated because I would cry, but there were very few tears.

Jason had this old, navy blue Polo brand T-shirt that he absolutely loved. Honestly, it was a rag. It was tattered and holey, but it was his favorite so he still wore it. It was one of those shirts that, no matter how much you washed it, still smelled as if it had been worn. He didn't wear it in public or anything, but he wore it frequently around the house or to do yard work. In fact, he wore it the day he painted the baby's room, and it had spots of brown and pink paint all over it. It became like my security blanket. Anytime during the day that I could catch a little rest, and at night, I would cling to it, bury my face in it, and just cry. It smelled of him, and I guess it kind of made me feel as though he was still there.

Sleeping or I guess I should say attempting to sleep, alone in a bed where I was used to sleeping next to someone, was hard. I hated it. I hated feeling alone. It was scary, sad, and depressing, and I hated it. These were seriously the longest, hardest, most depressing few days of my life. More family came to town, more friends stopped by to visit, and each visit and hug was like a brutal reminder of this horrible tragedy, relived over and over again. As I've said, my son and my unborn daughter were my saving grace, my reason for even getting out of bed each day. Jaren was taking everything in the best he could. Children are so matter-of-fact and accepting. If only adults had such simple faith this world would be a much better place. He knew that his dad had gone to heaven to be with God and Jesus. Period. Yes, he was sad and said he really missed him, but he seemed content with the idea of Jason being safe in heaven and our guardian angel.

As much of a nightmare as the scene of the accident was for me, I could not fathom what images might be in Jaren's head. He was there, he'd seen the whole thing, and he saw his dad unconscious. He had been through a lot, so when the question of whether to take him to the viewing at the funeral home arose, I was totally against it. I just did not feel like it was a good place for a four-year-old to be. However, after visiting with Pastor Dennis, I decided that maybe, just like adults, children need closure also, and maybe Jaren needed to see his dad this way as a final image, instead of the accident scene. It turned out to be a good decision to take him because it showed us yet another example of how God speaks to us. I am a firm believer that He speaks to us through children all the time.

Keep in mind that Jaren was a very energetic four-year-old boy at this time. He loved to run around, especially outside, and he loved to find "treasures" such as sticks, rocks, etc. His pockets were usually full of his outside treasures. The funeral home where the viewing was held had quite a few trees and nice landscaping, so as soon as Jaren jumped out of the car, he was off exploring. I was already emotionally and physically exhausted, so it was a bit irritating to me that he had already run off when that was clearly not what we were there for. I did not have the energy to chase him down, though, so I went on inside with my mom while my dad and Pastor Dennis stayed outside with him. Plus, I wanted some time to myself to view Jason for the first time since the accident and just be alone to process it all. I had been feeling a little guilty and remorseful that I had not taken more time with him the night he died. But then I guess, what good would it have done? I know it was just a body. I had no doubt in my mind that his spirit and soul were with Jesus. All sadness and grief aside, it did give me great peace to be confident and sure that Jason was in heaven. Even still, I guess I had to go through with the viewing, if not for myself, then for any family and friends who might come to pay their respects.

I have never been much of a fan of funerals. I had only been to a handful of them, and they honestly just always made me feel horrible. I understand the purpose and respect that, but I've just never liked feeling sad and watching how sad the family always appears to be. Yes, you can call it "a celebration of life," and for Christians it truly should be, as we know that our life on earth is only our temporary home and our ultimate goal is to live in eternity with Jesus. But I *really* have to work hard to convince myself that it should feel like a celebration.

Most of the funerals I had attended to date had been for unexpected, untimely deaths and were therefore, very, very sad. I had a grandpa die of a heart attack—sad. My grandma on my dad's side, whom I was extremely close to, died of lung cancer—sad. A friend in high school one year younger than me died in a fiery car accident, which also killed a well-known woman in our community—doubly sad. I went to a funeral of one of my younger brother's friends, who died as a result of massive head trauma from being attacked one night when he was in college—devastatingly sad.

Others were from more natural causes like old age, but my point is that funerals, in my experience, were just tough. But the reality is no one lives forever, and when it is our time to go, then so be it. Despite that fact, never in a million years did I imagine I would be planning and attending one for my thirty-one-year-old husband. I was truly dreading it, but then on the other hand I wanted it over. I had no idea what would come next, but I just wanted the ceremonial parts of Jason's death to be done and over.

I had absolutely no idea what he was going to look like. The cause of death was ruled "cardiac arrest due to massive head trauma and cervical spine fracture." Jason basically took the impact of the deer. I still, to this day, cannot believe the timing of the whole incident. Seriously, everything was timed perfectly. That oncoming car hit that deer in just enough time that it flew right into our truck as we passed by. I would really like to know, scientifically, the odds of that happening. Eventually, I accepted the fact that Jason did not survive, and it was a horrible, tragic freak accident, but I still often ponder the "what ifs?" What if Jaren had been injured or killed, or what if none of us had survived?

Once we were able to assess the truck, it appeared that the deer entered the windshield through the driver's side but then exited at a diagonal path out the back window behind the passenger's side, breaking out the backseat passenger side window in the process. The backseat passenger side is where Jaren was sitting. Ugh, it gives me chills and turns my stomach to think about it. It sickens me to even think that I could have lost both of them that night.

Later on, when questioned about the accident and what he remembered, Jaren said he saw the deer coming and he ducked down and put his blanket over his head. Friends, he was four-years-old.

The only explanation for it is Jesus. Again, the fact that I felt God's presence in helping me stop that moving vehicle and knowing that He protected Jaren and me, was the cause of a major struggle for me. Even with the strong faith that I had, I still could not grasp how He could protect Jaren and myself, yet take Jason at the same time. It has become one of those unanswered questions that I have just stopped asking and simply accepted.

I have since learned that a person can drive themselves crazy chasing down the whys and asking questions that they will never have answers to. During my grieving process I even went so far as to question what if I hadn't even gotten pregnant ... then there would not have been a baby shower to travel to, and we would not have been on the road that night, and so on. Grieving makes the mind do some pretty crazy things.

Chapter 11

Daddy's Feather

So how did Jason look? I was actually amazed. As I've said, I had no idea what to expect, since he suffered such massive head trauma. He had some facial bruising, but it was mostly on the left side, so with makeup and that side facing the inside of the casket, it really was not noticeable. He did have quite a bit of drainage from his ears so they did have to pack them with cotton to keep the drainage contained. Other than that, he looked just like Jason. He looked ready for a day at the golf course in his favorite navy-blue Denver Broncos polo and hideous orange cargo shorts. He would not have had it any other way. In fact, when we asked his cousins and closest friends to be pallbearers, we told them to also wear shorts and polo shirts. For a moment I felt as though I was in that nightmare again, and all I wanted was for him to just wake up and for everything to go back to normal.

I had somewhat drifted off into my own little world when I heard a little energetic voice hollering, "Mommy, Mommy, look what I found!" I snapped back into reality to find Jaren running toward me waving something in his hand. Keep in mind he had not seen

Jason yet, so that was really all I could think of, and I was a little panicked, as he ran toward me getting closer to the casket. He was so preoccupied by what he had to show me that he didn't really even notice Jason at first.

I composed myself, smiled, and asked, "What did you find, buddy?"

He responded, "A beautiful feather, Mommy." Tears filled my eyes again, as I instantly felt a strange, yet peaceful presence. Ironically, I had recently read somewhere that finding a feather was a sign of an angel. Some believe a feather is a communication from an angel letting you know that they are safe in heaven and that they are watching over and protecting you.

With tears streaming down my face I grabbed him, hugged him tight, and whispered, "It's a beautiful feather, baby."

Jaren loved to give gifts. Anytime a friend came over, he would always want them to have whatever toys of his were their favorites. You could see the joy on his face anytime he gave someone a gift. He loved to draw and color, so he often drew pictures for people as gifts. He really was not a selfish child at all despite being an only child for four years.

After showing me this beautiful feather and seeing how I admired it, he then asked, "Can I give it to Daddy, Mommy?" I felt as if my heart swelled ten times its normal size and was going to explode in my chest. I was speechless.

To my relief, Pastor Dennis stepped in and took over for a while. He was and is truly a man of God. God spoke through him a lot during this whole situation, and this was no different. At this point Jaren had still not seen Jason, so Pastor Dennis took this opportunity to ask Jaren if he would like to see his dad. Jaren nodded, and Pastor then proceeded to prepare Jaren for what he was about to see. I stood there in awe as Pastor chose each word very carefully and did a wonderful job of explaining things to Jaren. I know that he knew that I did not have the composure to do it. Pastor Dennis was "Jesus with skin on" that day, and I was thankful for him being there with us.

I really had no idea what Jaren's reaction would be to seeing Jason at the funeral home. The kid was four, for goodness' sake, and had just lost his daddy in a horrific accident. I was again reminded that God was truly with us that day as Jaren was so mature about the situation. He didn't get upset, and he didn't cry; he just slowly walked up to the casket and stood there without saying anything for a few minutes. Then the "why" questions started rolling in. The two that come to mind were (1) "Is he just sleeping? It looks like he is just sleeping," and (2) "If daddy is in heaven, then why can I see him right here?" The mind of a child fascinates me.

Again, Pastor Dennis stepped in and worked his magic with his explanations. It was as if Jaren just "got it." Kids are so matter-of-fact and resilient. I've said it before, but if only adults could sometimes think like children in certain instances, the world might be a much better place.

Recall that Jaren was really into giving gifts, and remember the feather he found? In true Jaren fashion, he asked again, "Can I give Daddy this feather I found?" I told him, sure, if he really wanted to. However, after just standing there and thinking for a few minutes, he decided that he thought he wanted to just keep the feather. He said that it was a very special feather, that it would always make him think of his daddy, and that Daddy was an angel in heaven.

We all know what the attention span of a four-year-old is, so it was no surprise that Jaren had had about enough of the viewing. By this time various family members had arrived, so there were plenty of legs to chase him around. I was already exhausted at this point, both mentally and physically, so I went to the back of the room to sit and rest. Ever since the accident, no one wanted to leave me alone, so when my mom saw me excuse myself to take a breather, she followed and sat with me.

My mom is another prime example of Jesus with skin on. She has the strongest faith of anyone I know and a vast knowledge of the Bible. She has always been my go-to person with "God questions," and she always knows how to make me feel better in any situation. She was and is an outstanding role model for me and my brothers and really anyone who knows her. She has taught me countless things, but she has always instilled in me that no matter what you are going through, first of all remember God is with you, and secondly there is always someone else fighting a harder battle then you.

So as we were sitting there at the funeral home for a viewing of my husband, I burst into tears. Through the sobs I said to my mom, "You always say that no matter how bad a situation is, it could always be worse. Mom, I don't know how this could be worse."

At this point she was crying too, and all she could do was hug me and say, "I know." Even my mom—my mentor, my rock, and the woman I could always count on for answers—did not know how to explain this.

This is the next place in the story where God steps in. People had started to arrive for the viewing, most of them good friends or family. Not five minutes after Mom and I had our conversation, a gentleman walked in alone. I knew who he was, and I knew that he was a client of Jason's at the accounting firm, but other than that, I did not know him well. He walked to the front of the room, spent his time viewing the body, greeted a few people he knew, and then approached me. He shook my hand and gave me his condolences and then he left. My mom was standing with me the entire time, and when he left, I turned and looked at her. The look on both of our faces must have been priceless. I am not sure if shock and awe are good descriptive words, but I was definitely shocked to see him and also in awe of the fact that he came to pay his respects to someone he barely knew.

You see, on September 4, 2007, not quite a year earlier, this man's wife and oldest daughter were both killed in a car accident. As if that weren't enough, his daughter was newly married and pregnant. I remember when the accident happened and the effect it had on the community. I also remember thinking at that time how devastated the poor man must be to lose his wife, daughter, and unborn grandchild in a single horrific day. I could not imagine what that would be like and of course thought, *I just hope nothing like that ever happens to me.*

I had the utmost respect and admiration for him at that moment. Here was a man who had suffered multiple losses not even a year ago, and yet he came to pay his respects to me in my loss. Do you see where God is in this? Still, to this day, the story gives me chills. I use it all the time as an example of a situation where no matter how hard times can be, someone else is having or has had harder times. Talk about asked and answered messages from God. And this was just the beginning of my realization that God truly does speak to me, maybe not literally, but He definitely gets His point across one way or another.

Chapter 12

Funeral Day

I might have nicely mentioned that I did not care for funerals much. I was trying to be nice. To be quite honest, I hate funerals. I understand and respect their purpose, but that does not mean I have to like them. You can imagine how much I was dreading this one, my husband's funeral. I still could not wrap my head around it. I just wanted it over and done with. I really did not want to have to face all those people, knowing how sorry they all felt for me and our family.

Let me take a second to remind you that it was summer, August now, and it was hot. It was *so* hot, and I was *so* pregnant! As if I was not miserable enough the way it was, the summer heat did not help one bit. I feel sorry for everyone who had to be around me; I am sure I was not the most pleasant person. I was miserably uncomfortable, sad, and grouchy, not to mention other unpleasant feelings, and I needed something to wear for a funeral. I was in no mood to get dressed up, but it had to be done. The day had come—funeral day.

I struggled just to get dressed that morning, knowing what was ahead of me. Luckily, I had a dress that fit. Thank goodness for Target and rayon/spandex blends. I still felt like a whale, but it would have to do. Besides, I would wear it only once and then throw it away. I would never again wear a dress that I wore eight months pregnant to my husband's funeral.

It's not like it was a Christmas dress or Easter dress or fancy little black dress that I might wear again. This was my funeral dress, and I never wanted to look at it again after that day. I was reminded of the outfit I was wearing the day of the accident and how I made them just throw it all away at the hospital. I never wanted to see it again. I didn't want to take the chance of having any material reminders of that day whatsoever.

A funeral is not just a funeral when you are the family of the deceased. It is much more than the thirty-minute ceremony. A funeral for family is almost like a seminar with lots of crying and hugging. You even get an agenda: 9:00 family meet in church parlor, 9:30 reading of the flowers and memorials for family, 10:00 family reconvenes in parlor, 10:30 family is seated and service begins. Then there is the graveside service; then reconvene back at church for lunch, greet visitors, and on and on.

And so it began. The reading of the flowers and memorials left me in awe at the thoughtfulness of people. It is truly amazing how many people sent flowers or memorials. Once the reading was over, the funeral director announced that the family could have some time to view the casket and say their final goodbyes. Oh my goodness, shot to the heart hearing "final goodbyes." I believe a broken heart is a real thing, and I had one. I suddenly felt sick to my stomach. I just stayed seated in the pew.

When everyone had pretty much cleared out and the only ones left in the room were my parents, my brothers and myself, my mom nudged me that it was time. She took my hand and walked with me to the back of the church where the casket was. There we stood, all in a line, my dad and mom, then me, and then my two brothers. There were no words, just tears. This was it, the "final goodbye."

There Jason lay in his orange and blue, looking as if he should be headed out for a round of golf. Next to him I had placed a picture of our last sonogram of the baby. Since Jaren had decided against giving him the feather he found at the funeral home, he said he wanted to give him something else. He went home that day, went to his room searching for something to give his daddy, and came out with the book *Goodnight Moon*. It was his favorite book, and Jason read it to him almost every night. He even drew pictures inside it of Jason as an angel in heaven. So I let him place the book in the casket also.

And then it all just hit me. I dropped to my knees and lay across his chest, hugging him and crying. Crying for it to not be real, crying that I couldn't go on without him. I just kept saying, "I can't do this, I can't do this." My mom once told me that the image of me lying across his chest hugging him and crying, while each of my family members had a hand on my back in an attempt to comfort and support me, will forever be imbedded in her memory.

Chapter 13

"Celebration" of Life

I really am not a selfish person, but it seems as if I have been writing about the funeral as though I was the only one it affected. That was not the case at all. Jason was loved by so many people. We both grew up in very close families and family was very important to us. I know that his family felt devastated as well. Both sets of his grandparents were still alive and were there along with all his aunts, uncles and cousins on both sides. Everyone was still experiencing a lot of disbelief that it was even real. I felt so awful for all of them but especially his dad, mom, and sister. I was experiencing what it was like to lose a spouse, but here they were trying to cope with losing a son and a brother. It just all seemed so unfair. Why did this have to happen? Why DO bad things happen to such good people? Despite the grief that all his family members were coping with, they were all so concerned with how I was doing. It is just such an awful reason for family to have to get together if you ask me. But for now, it was what it was and we were all there together in a room waiting to be ushered into a sanctuary full of people for what is often optimistically referred to as a "celebration of life". I, for one, did not feel anywhere near celebratory.

I am told that more than five hundred people attended that day, which is truly amazing and speaks very highly of the person Jason was. Unfortunately, at the time, in my grieving, bad-attitude state of mind, all I saw was a packed room full of people watching as a devastated family and a widowed, pregnant single mom walked in, feeling sorry for us. But in retrospect, it was a wonderful tribute to Jason to have that many people gathered to pay their respects.

It was really a nice service, despite the fact that Jaren was—well, a four-year-old boy who did not like to sit still and found it more entertaining to climb on, over, and under the altar rails. It was slightly distracting to say the least, but I also did not have the energy to care or to chase him. I wanted the service as simple and quick as possible. I loved music, but Jason was really not the musical type, so I knew he would not want a big to-do of music. Unless of course it was Air Supply or the Beatles. I swear he had the musical tastes of someone forty years his elder. I could hardly stand to ride in a car with him because of the radio stations he listened to. Anyway, I decided that congregational singing would be sufficient; I had no idea whom I could ask who might feel comfortable singing at a sad time like this.

I've already mentioned that I will forever be grateful to Pastor Dennis for all he did during this time. He had only been in Scott City a month or two at most, but he seemed to know us all quite well just by spending a little time with us. When he first arrived as pastor of our church, he made it a point to visit each Sunday school class just to get acquainted with everyone. The Sunday that he visited our class, we happened to be sharing testimonies, so he got to hear Jason's. Little did he know it would be material for his first funeral as pastor of our church. He did an amazing job and truly made it sound as if he had known us for years.

What do I hate more than funerals? Cemeteries. Just being honest. I really don't know why, either. I guess the thought of putting a body in a box and then burying that box deep in the ground simply bothers me. I honestly wish that when we died, our entire body ascended into heaven along with our soul. It would just be so much easier. Plus it makes death final, and you will never ever see the body again.

Thankfully, the graveside service was fairly short. It was something like 103 degrees out that day, so *miserable* is an understatement. I was feeling terribly sick by this time and just wanted the day to be over. But I knew we still had friends and family to greet back at the church. Again, I was amazed and truly touched by the people who came for the funeral. Many friends came from long distances to be there, and it really meant a great deal to me. All the hugs really did give me strength. It also made me proud of the man Jason was that so many people wanted to be there. With over five hundred people in attendance, it was the largest funeral I had ever been to.

Talk about a long and exhausting day. Once we were finally home, I needed to rest. I was physically, mentally, and emotionally drained. For a while I even felt like I might be having contractions and feared I was going into labor. I think it was just all the stress of the day, because once I was able to rest, the feeling subsided.

Chapter 14

Now What Do I Do?

Some say funerals bring closure. They are pretty final, but I was far from feeling closure. The first few days after someone dies, it seems as if something always needs to be done in preparation for the funeral. Then once the funeral is over and the family all leaves, then what? I was lost and broken.

Being pregnant didn't help one bit either, or having a four-year-old, for that matter. Luckily, Jaren still went to daycare, so that helped a little bit. My mom was staying with me too, which was a huge help, but the days she went to work and Jaren went to daycare, I found myself with my head buried in a pillow or not able to get off the couch because I was so sad and depressed. It was truly awful. I cannot even begin to describe how much I was hurting, but there were days when I thought there were only two options in this world that would make the pain go away. The first was if Jason could come back. Since obviously that wasn't happening, the second was if I were dead too. Yes, I said it. I admit it, I had those thoughts.

I have never really understood suicide and how someone could choose that option, but I can honestly say that I have a greater appreciation for what such deep pain and depression can make you think about. Fortunately, I did not choose that route, and I wholeheartedly believe that it was because of my faith and many people's prayers for me. Even though I was not in the state of mind at the time to spend a lot of time in prayer, thankfully I had an army of prayer warriors backing me. To be honest, I wasn't exactly sure how to feel about faith at that point. I was probably so numb that I wasn't feeling a whole lot except pain and pregnancy.

I did feel compelled to go to church that Sunday after the funeral; it just felt like where I needed to be. It could have been because that was the last place I saw Jason's body the day before, but now I believe that it was God guiding me. My parents went with me, and we sat clear in the back so that very few people even realized we were there. I felt the best I had felt all week that morning in church. I felt as though God had sent the Holy Spirit to wrap me up in a big hug for that hour.

Good friends of ours were singing that day as well. They sang "Come to Jesus" by Chris Rice and dedicated it to Jason. They did not know I was at church until after the service. They both said that had they known, there was no way they could have made it through the song and kept their composure. Their music was truly a blessing to me that day. It gave me a sense of peace, even if only for a few minutes. The words were perfect and touching. It is truly an amazing song. The final line of the song says, "Fly to Jesus, fly to Jesus, fly to Jesus and live," and for a few moments that was exactly how I pictured things … Jason flying to Jesus.

Chapter 15

Life Goes On

Life was suddenly weird. I was used to a routine, and then, *bam*, one day it all changed. Obviously, I needed to take time off from work, even though I had maternity leave coming up anyway. There was no way I was in the right frame of mind to be around people, especially at the place where my husband had just died.

So my days were pretty boring. This was before I joined Facebook or any of the other time-sucking social media sites, so I didn't have that to occupy my time. The days Jaren was home, I would force myself to go outside or take him to the park. I really didn't want to be at my house. I would watch the clock and wait for 5:00 p.m. to roll around, and then I would imagine that Jason would be coming home from work as he always had. It was miserable. Luckily, despite it being August, the weather was unseasonably mild (which I credit to Jason), so being outside actually did make me feel better.

I was exhausted, but I couldn't sleep. I am one who doesn't sleep well when I am alone, and let me tell you, I felt very alone. I actually asked Jaren if he would sleep with me just to have someone there.

He rarely slept with us, as I was not a fan of co-sleeping with kids because I never slept well. But I remember that on the rare occasion when Jaren came to our room, Jason gladly picked him up and put him in between us. If I complained or questioned him about it, then he would always sing a few bars of that song by Billy Dean, "Let Them Be Little," and specifically the part that says, "Let them sleep in the middle." Still makes me smile to this day when I think about that. Jaren was such a good sport and agreed to sleep with Mommy. But then, bless his heart, one night at bedtime, he looked at me with his sweet little face and said, "Mommy, could I please sleep in my own bed?" So he did, which was fine, because I had the baby shortly thereafter and would have had him go back to his room anyway.

As much as I do not care for visiting cemeteries, I found myself going out to visit Jason's grave quite often. I would sit at his graveside and talk to him. I cried a lot, but it was good ugly crying. It felt good to let some of the emotion out and not worry about anyone being around to witness it or feel sorry for me. Another thing I really hated about the whole situation was constantly sensing that everyone felt sorry for me. Don't get me wrong; I truly appreciated everyone's concern, and I know all they wanted to do was help, but it was still awkward, and I hated the attention.

I was lost. I was eight months pregnant with a baby we'd tried for over two years to have. I was the mom of a four-year-old boy, and I was a widow. These kids would have no father. How could this be the plan?

I had so many questions, so many "Why?"s. I was confused and wanted answers. At this point in time, I began to realize that God truly does speak to me, maybe not literally, but He definitely gets His point across one way or another.

God clearly spoke to me a week or so after Jason's passing. He spoke to me in a dream. I had heard of people having dreams of loved ones lost before, but I guess I never expected to have one, let alone so soon. In my dream Jason was sitting on a tall gold throne, and I was kneeling at his feet. He put his hand on me and said, "Everything is going to be all right." He then proceeded to give me instructions on how to take care of the finances, which was hilarious to me because I had no clue about our finances and was very stressed about that. Jason was the accountant, and he took care of all that. When I woke up after having that dream, I felt a calming peace, and I knew this was God's message that Jason was in heaven and that everything would be OK.

So where do I go from here? I begged and pleaded with God for the answers to many questions. This is not at all how I had imagined my life. Having realized that, I started to learn that much of life truly is out of our control. This was also when I truly understood and appreciated the power of prayer. I learned that prayer isn't just about you, yourself praying, it's about people praying for other people. Have you ever heard someone say they felt your prayers, or have *you* ever experienced that feeling? I did. My family had countless people praying for us, people I did not even know. It was amazing. Having been through this situation, I learned that people badly want to help. Maybe you know someone you wanted to help but didn't know how. Sometimes the greatest thing you can do is just pray for them.

A lot of my life at this point became a blur. I was just trying to survive and get through the days. I was pregnant and miserable and sad. If not for my son and my close family and friends, it's hard to say what I would have done. I can honestly say now that the most important things in my life that got me through this time were what I like to refer to as F^3 (*F* cubed): my faith, family, and friends.

As I had mentioned, Jason took care of all the bills and finances so that was a major stressor for me. Come to find out, we had some pretty major credit card debt of which I was totally unaware. Plus now there were insurance claims to make and medical bills, and frankly I did not want to deal with any of it. And then there was the issue of life insurance. I carried a small amount through my job, and we also had an accident policy through Aflac, but aside from that I was unaware of any life insurance that Jason had on himself. All I knew was when he switched jobs, a benefits package did not exactly come with the new job, so I knew he didn't have a policy through his work. I completely took it for granted that he took care of all the finances and wished then that I had been more involved. It definitely would have prevented a lot of stress.

Luckily, I did know where the filing cabinet was and knew that he kept every receipt, bill, and credit card statement. I guess I can thank the accountant in him for that. My parents, being almost as stressed about my financial situation as I was, encouraged me to go through the filing cabinet and see if I could find any information on a life insurance policy. Lo and behold, I came across a file that contained what appeared to be a life insurance policy through some sort of accounting association that he was a member of. There was also a copy of a check that Jason had written when he took out the policy, which ironically happened to have been just six months before. A small wave of hope came over me, but I wanted to call the number on the documents just to make sure. Tears filled my eyes, and I was overwhelmed with relief as the woman on the other end of the phone confirmed that it was, indeed, a legitimate and current life insurance policy. As devastating as it was to lose Jason and have to actually use a life insurance policy, I am thankful that he had it and that financially my kids and I would be OK.

After a few weeks had passed I decided that I needed to try to get back into some sort of routine. I thought maybe if I went back to work, it would occupy my time and my mind. I truly loved my job and, more importantly, the people I worked with, so I thought maybe it would be good for me. Plus, I still had a few weeks left to go in my pregnancy, and didn't want to use up all my vacation time before I even went on maternity leave. It did prove to be really good for me. I did have a few breakdowns when something triggered a memory, but overall it was good to be around people.

Chapter 16

Reaching Out

It was mid-August now, and my sister-in-law Linda, Jason's sister, called me one day. She was due around the same time, so we had enjoyed being pregnant together and visiting often to compare pregnancies. She was having a really rough day that day. Not only was she missing her brother and still trying to process it all, but she had received upsetting news about one of her good friends from college. She told me that this friend had passed out in her bathroom and was unresponsive when her husband found her. Apparently, she had been diagnosed with a heart condition that they thought was being controlled with medication. She said they were able to revive her and that they flew her to KU med in Kansas City, but the doctors were not very hopeful that she would regain consciousness or have any brain activity. On top of being sad about her friend, she was very concerned for her friend's husband and their two small kids, who were seven and two. Even though I did not know these people, I felt devastated for them, and I told Linda that I would pray for them and asked her to keep me posted.

Sadly, her next phone call two weeks later was to tell me that her friend, Cari, had passed away on August 29, almost one month to the day after Jason died. Having just lost my spouse and the father of my children, I could imagine the horrific pain this man must be feeling. I asked Linda for his address because after everything everyone had done for me in my time of loss, I felt compelled to reach out to his family and extend my sympathy. It truly was amazing how people did reach out. Aside from family, friends, and practically the entire communities of Scott City as well as my hometown, Healy, and Jason's, Atwood, I had people send sympathy cards and memorials whom I did not even know and who did not even know me. One woman, whom I will never forget, sent me a card and stamps. She wrote me the kindest message and told me that she had also lost her spouse in a deer-related accident. She expressed how much her faith had helped her through that tragedy and said that she had recently remarried. It was truly a message of hope for me, in fact, the first time I even remember feeling hope at all since Jason's death. Her card inspired me to want to reach out to others in their time of need who were on a similar path.

Consequently, something kept telling me I needed to send Linda's friend's husband a sympathy card. As I sat down one day to write the card, I just sat and stared at the blank page. I really didn't know what to say. So I said a little prayer that God would give me the words to send to this grieving man and his kids, and this is what I came up with:

> Scott and family,
>
> First of all, I just want to express my deepest sympathy and tell you that you and your family have been in my thoughts and prayers. I know we do not know each other. I am Linda (Kanak) Bolen's sister-in-law. Her brother, Jason, was my husband.
>
> I am not going to say that I know how you feel, because only you really know how you feel—but I do

know what you are going through in a way. I know how bad it hurts and how hard it is to understand and how unfair it is and how much we are missing them. Everyone, friends and family, are all so supportive, and we thank God for them—but when they ask what they can do, all I can think is for them to bring back our loved one. That is the only thing that would make this all better. I am so sad for my kids, as I am sure you are as well.

I wish I had the perfect, comforting thing to say, but all I can do is just hold tight to my memories. I have relied heavily on my faith, family, and friends, which has been a big help but doesn't always ease the pain.

If you ever feel like talking to someone who has been through what you are going through, please let me know. I hope and pray that things will get better with time. We have to go on, as hard as it is—especially for our kids and the rest of our family.

Once again, I am so very sorry, and seriously, if you feel like talking—even to a stranger—I am here.

And that was that. I included a memorial donation as well as my email address and phone number, and I sent the card. As I recall, it was the first week of September at this point. I was getting very close to having the baby; my due date was August 31, so I was already overdue. To say I was miserable is an understatement. I was experiencing many different emotions. I did not even want to have this baby. I mean I wanted to have it—obviously I didn't want to be pregnant anymore— but I was just so sad about the whole situation. To go through two and a half years of trying to conceive, then conceiving only to lose my husband and baby's father just weeks before giving birth, was just way too much for me to handle. My doctor was extremely worried about both me and the baby due to the severe emotional stress I had been under. I had lost fifteen pounds since the accident, and all I could do during my weekly appointments was sit in the exam room and cry. I was taking the highest dose of an antidepressant that I could safely take. I was worried that it was not good for the baby, but I simply could not function without it. I honestly did not know if I had the strength, either mentally or physically, to give birth. I was very adamant that I did not want to have labor induced, so my doctor agreed to let me go past my due date. But after another week and a half and still no real labor, he convinced me to go through with the induction and scheduled it for September 10. I remembered that with Jaren, the actual scheduling of induction put me into labor, so I was really hoping for that in this case as well. And that is exactly what happened.

Chapter 17

Welcome, Beautiful Baby Girl

My water broke around 4:30 a.m. on the same day I was scheduled for induction. I was supposed to be at the hospital at 6 a.m. anyway, so I just waited and went as planned. Even though I was laboring on my own, the doctor still wanted to give me Pitocin just to be sure there was no regression of labor.

On the outside I was holding it together pretty well, but I was actually a nervous wreck. I have a tendency to let my mind wander and think of every possible horrible scenario that might happen. You know, all those "what ifs." I had endless thoughts streaming through my head. I was sad that Jason was not going to be there for the birth of his daughter. I was nervous that something would go wrong during labor and delivery and that something bad was going to happen to either me or the baby. I had already decided that I did not want to be alone in the delivery room, so I had asked my mom to be with me.

Labor was progressing nicely, but my discomfort grew as stronger and stronger contractions came more frequently, so I finally asked for an epidural. I had planned to get one anyway; I had had one with my son, and it was amazing. It did, however, seem to slow my labor, so I wanted to wait this time until I absolutely couldn't stand the pain any longer. My first epidural, in Hays, was a piece of cake, and in fact I could not even tell when the anesthesiologist administered it. Then, talk about instant relief.

This time, however, was not even close to the same experience. For one thing, the nurse anesthetist was likely nervous, considering everything I had already been through as well as my being a coworker. I could tell exactly when he stuck that needle in my back, and even worse, I could tell that it was not in the right place. Almost immediately, I got very light-headed, sweaty, and nauseated. It was the worst sick feeling I had ever experienced. My blood pressure significantly dropped, and they had to lay me down. I thought I was dying; this was it, my worst fear. I prayed that the horrible feeling would pass and that everything would be OK.

After a few minutes, I started to come around and feel better. Hesitantly, I agreed to let him try again, and this time it went just fine. Instead of a continuous drip like the one I had with my first delivery, this was just a bolus that would only last a couple hours and have to be readministered should it wear off before I delivered. But for now, I was comfortable and back to patiently waiting. Around 10:00 a.m. I started to feel a little uncomfortable as the first dose started to wear off, and then I remember feeling a sensation as if the baby stretched her body out and straightened her legs, trying to push herself down. It was the craziest feeling! I told my mom about it and said I felt it was almost time to have this baby. The nurses went ahead and called the doctor, who came right away. My instincts were right: I was fully dilated, and she was ready to make her way into the world. Oh my goodness, what a wave of emotion, but again the thing I prayed for above all was for us both to be healthy and unharmed.

Once the doctor and nurses got everything prepared and we all got into position, it literally took me two pushes. Then came the sweetest sound of a newborn baby's cry. It brings tears to my eyes just recalling it and writing about it. The nurses and respiratory therapist took her right away to check her over thoroughly while the doctor attended to me. The baby checked out great, and they quickly had her all cleaned up and ready to meet her mama.

Words cannot do justice to the feelings that came over me as I held my daughter for the first time. She was beautiful and absolutely perfect, and it was if I could see Jason in her eyes. I am so glad we had already chosen a name before he died. Since Jaren had the same initials and middle name as Jason, we wanted our daughter to have my initials and middle name. We chose the name Lynsi Diane, and it fit her perfectly.

At that moment I overflowed with gratitude to my doctor, all the staff, and especially my mom. I don't think I could have done it without her, and I was so thankful to have her there. She later told me that to be present for the birth of her granddaughter was one of the most amazing experiences she has ever had, especially considering the circumstances. I also think that this was one of the many days since Jason's accident that I can honestly say I felt lifted up in prayer. I know there were many people praying for me and for the birth of a healthy baby, and I was grateful because it truly gave me the strength I needed.

Now that baby Lynsi was finally here, I could not wait for Jaren to meet his little sister. He had preschool that morning, and my dad was to pick him up at noon and bring him to the hospital. I was so happy to see that little guy when he came bebopping in the room that day. I was holding Lynsi, and he jumped right up on the bed beside me and gave her a kiss on the head. Even though I was still sad, at that moment I was filled with an overwhelming sense of joy and gratitude for these two children who were truly gifts from God.

The birth of a child is supposed to be a happy occasion. And for the most part it was. But I could not help but miss Jason and wish so badly that he might be there in person. I truly felt his presence and like to think that he was watching over us, but that still did not change the fact that I wished he were there in person. As long as I had visitors or family with me that day, I was fine. It wasn't until Jason's dad, Joe, arrived that I broke down.

I was actually alone with the baby that evening when Joe arrived. He was holding the baby and admiring her when suddenly a huge wave of emotion swept over me, and I burst into tears. I just kept saying, "He should be here." Joe tried his best to console me by agreeing with me and also by saying how proud Jason would be and how special Lynsi was and how he would want me to stay strong and take good care of our two children. It had to be incredibly hard for him too.

I did not really want to spend the night in the hospital alone, so my mom had planned for her and Jaren to stay with me. Containing him in a hospital room and trying to get him to be quiet and go to sleep was a lost cause. So I finally encouraged her to just take him to our house for the night. I said I would be fine.

But I wasn't fine. Nighttime had been the hardest for me, and this night was no different. It was just me and the baby, and I felt very alone. I think I cried most of the night. It was nights like that where I tried to reflect on Psalm 30:5 (NRSV), which says, "For his anger is but for a moment; his favor is for a lifetime. Weeping may linger for the night, but joy comes with the morning." I kept telling myself over and over, "Joy comes in the morning," and once that first night after giving birth had passed, I did feel better the next morning. Plus, I was hopeful that we could go home that day. One night in a short hospital bed was enough for me.

The next day was September 11, 2008. It was now the seventh anniversary of the 9/11 terrorist attacks. I will always remember that day and that year. I was working at the hospital in Hays the day it happened. A waiting room with a TV was near the area I worked in.

I happened to be escorting a patient to the waiting room and caught a glimpse of what was happening on the TV. I couldn't take my eyes off it. It was unbelievable, to say the least. It was definitely an event that changed our country and many lives forever. It was just two months before Jason and I were to be married. We were supposed to then fly to Jamaica for our honeymoon, so I remember being extremely nervous about flying.

Anyway, back to 2008; of course, the 9/11 anniversary was all over the news and radio, which triggered these memories for me. That led to me reminiscing back to 2001 and our wedding. Although it was a beautiful memory in theory, it made me sad. Honestly, when you say those vows, "till death do us part," do you really think it will be after only a few years and at such a young age? I sure didn't.

There is so much in life we truly take for granted until it is gone or over. Of course, everyone will always have a few regrets and wish that they'd had a chance to say certain things or even just to say goodbye. There are things I do regret, but ultimately, I had to learn to let them go. There was absolutely nothing I could do about the past, and no amount of regret or wishing I could go back was going to change my present situation. I knew that I just needed to continue to hold tight to my faith and hope and pray that God would guide me and heal me. But I sure wanted Him to hurry up, because this was almost too hard to handle.

Chapter 18

Waiting for a "Godincidence"

Waiting is hard. Being patient is hard. Trusting God's timing is hard. Life is hard. These were all truths I had been pondering since the accident. After the accident and up to this point it seemed as if all I did was wait. Wait to find out how he was doing, wait for that first night to end, wait for the funeral, then after that was all over, my next hurdle was waiting for the baby to come. So now that she was here, what else did I have to wait for? Waiting for her arrival at least gave me a little sense of something to look forward to. But as sad as it sounds, now that she was here, what did I have to look forward to?

Lynsi was the most amazing baby, which really helped. I think God knew that I could only handle so much at this point, so He intervened and gave me a really good baby. He knew I needed rest, so He made her a good sleeper—a noisy sleeper, but a good sleeper. When we first came home, I put her in a bassinet next to my bed. Her room was just down the hall, but I liked having my babies close, especially as newborns. But holy cow, was she noisy. She would grunt and moan and snore, and you know when they are newborns, every little move or noise wakes a nervous mama. It wasn't long before I had to just put her in her crib in her room so that I could get some much-needed sleep.

My mom was still staying with me for now, but I sensed that she was getting a bit antsy to be back in her routine at home. I can't say that I blame her, as it had been basically a month and a half that she lived with me. I don't know what I would have done without her. She is the most amazing person and mom in the world as far as I am concerned. And she is the most giving and selfless person I know. She has been my mentor and a wonderful example to me, and I *wish* there was a way I could ever express my gratitude to her or repay her.

She was by my side every step of the way, from the accident to the funeral, Lynsi's birth, and beyond. She stayed strong for me, even though she was grieving the loss as well. Some days I was bitter and selfish and felt like I was the only one grieving, but the reality was that there were many people grieving for Jason. Aside from grieving, as a parent, Mom wanted so badly to be able to fix me and take my pain way. As a parent myself, I fully understand that we hate to see our children upset or hurting, and we long to fix or take away whatever is causing the pain.

I happened to be reading a book on grieving at the time, and it talked about this exact subject. The author was very supportive to the grief-stricken, though, in saying that you will have many people around you, most likely close loved ones, who will want to try and fix you. But the challenge is that you either cannot be fixed or don't want to be fixed at this point. All you want is to just know that you have their support and their listening ear. Ah, I could so relate to that! I remember one day I was feeling very depressed and down, and I was being very negative about life and complaining about how much it all hurt. I could tell that my mom was becoming extremely frustrated with me until finally she burst out: "You need to stop being so cynical."

Talk about a slap in the face! Up to this point my mom had been nothing but supportive, and now she was lecturing me. Having just read the passage I described, I whipped out that book, slammed it down in front of her, and pointed to the page, saying, "Here, you need to read this." I cannot even describe the look that came across her face as she read it. Tears filled her eyes, and she instantly just hugged me and started apologizing. We were embracing and crying, and all I could keep saying was "Mom, right now I can't be fixed, but I still need you to be here for me." I told her that some days I just needed to vent what was on my heart and mind or else I might go crazy.

My mom will attest to this day that that little encounter between us and her reading that passage completely changed her. She had been a parent for over thirty years, but that day she learned a very valuable lesson that would completely change the way she interacted not only with her children but with anyone who was faced with a trial.

All that aside, still it was time for my mom to leave. The reality was, she had her own life, and I needed a little tough love to get on with mine. So it was best that she got back to her life. Luckily, my parents just lived twenty-four miles away, and she worked in Scott City, so I still saw her all the time, and I actually spent a lot of time in Healy at their house.

Some days it was just good to get out of my house. There were so many constant reminders of Jason in the house. Sometimes they were good reminders and sparked good memories. Other times, they triggered sadness and depression. One day I sat rocking Lynsi and staring at our pictures on the wall. He was just staring back at me as I replayed everything that had happened. I was angry, and I wished with everything in me that he was still there, not just for me but to meet his daughter and be a father to his children. I felt so badly that he'd been robbed of that.

But then I had to remind myself that he was in heaven, and wasn't that the ultimate goal in life? I pictured him the way I saw him in my dream and felt a sense of peace and was happy for him. I imagine heaven to be the most amazing, indescribable place, and boy, was he lucky to be there. It's just frustrating that it's so hard for those of us left here on earth without them, missing them.

I've mentioned that I am not much of a cemetery visitor. However, on days when I had had enough and just needed to get out of the house and have some time to myself, I felt drawn to visit Jason's grave. I had not been out there since Lynsi's birth, so I decided I would go out and take to his grave a picture of her and a picture of Jaren holding her. I was feeling especially sad that day, so spending some time alone "talking" to Jason was just what I needed. Only what I intended to be some alone time ended up being one of those times in my life where I know God places people along our path for a reason.

I was sitting at Jason's grave telling him all about Lynsi, among other things. Tears streamed down my face as the pain of missing him along with postpartum hormones consumed me. I happened to catch something moving out of the corner of my eye, so I looked up and saw a woman on a bicycle riding into the cemetery. *Great*, I thought; *I hope she doesn't see me and minds her own business*. When I realized who it was, I knew that she was there to visit her mother-in-law's grave, which was right next to Jason's, so there was probably no chance of avoiding her.

I wiped my eyes and tried to compose myself as she approached me. I knew who she was, but I can't say I knew her well. She was a nurse at the hospital, so I was mostly acquainted with her from there, but her family was also well known in the community as owners of the flower shop and greenhouse in town.

She greeted me and then sat right down beside me and put her arm around me. At first, I thought, *Here we go, someone else who wants so badly to comfort me and help me but really has no idea what to do or say.* Boy, was I wrong. I learned a major lesson that day. You should never take for granted what people may have been through, just because you have never heard about it.

She started with small talk like "How ya doing? How's the baby? I'm so sorry." What she said next really caught me off guard. "You know, I lost my first husband too." Whoa, I wasn't sure how to respond to that. I had no idea. I knew that she had an older daughter with a different last name and that she was married now with two other daughters that shared her same name, but I guess I never really thought much about it. Sadly, when people have children with different last names, we often assume that they were previously divorced or never married. See what assuming gets us. *Ugh.*

I felt bad that I didn't know this about her, but at the same time I instantly felt great comfort in her embrace and her words. She shared her story with me and told me that it took ten years but that she had found love again; she remarried and had two more children. Her story definitely gave me hope, although I couldn't imagine what the next day of my life would bring, let alone the next ten years. I did know that I didn't want to feel this horrible pain for ten years. I think she could sense that and continued to reassure me that God would comfort and heal me.

I totally and completely believe in what I like to call *Godincidences.* I don't believe there are coincidences in life. Was it a coincidence that she just happened to ride her bike out to the cemetery at the exact same time I was there on that specific day? I don't believe so. I believe it was perfectly orchestrated by God and that she was His messenger that day, sending me a message of comfort and hope to remind me that I was not alone. It was what I needed that day, and I am sure she has no idea how much her time spent with me that day impacted me.

Chapter 19

Life-Changing Email

Aside from feeding, changing, and playing dress-up with my new baby girl, and trying to entertain my busy son, my days were spent trying to tie up loose ends left by the accident. It was overwhelming, to say the least. Luckily, most of the credit card companies and other agencies I had to contact were sympathetic and helpful once I told them the situation. It took all my strength not to burst into tears every time I had to give my reason for calling. I am thankful that I really did not have any issues at all, and I had to deal with *a lot* of different companies from credit cards and car and life insurance to student loans and eBay.

Yes, eBay. Remember, Jason was an eBay freak, to put it nicely. One might say he was something of a golf club broker. He would search auctions for golf clubs that he knew were valuable but for which the seller just had vague descriptions or poor-quality pictures. He would get them for a steal and then either turn around and sell them to a friend or on eBay or keep them. He could have had his own pro shop. He bought a plethora of other things too, but mostly golf or Denver Broncos memorabilia.

When he died, he had eight eBay auctions ongoing. Because I knew how much they meant to him, I went ahead and finished out his auctions and shipped the items to the buyers. Crazy, I know, but it was truly a passion of his, and he would have been crushed to get negative feedback. It was really the only reason he was ever online. Social media was not that popular yet, and neither he nor I had jumped on that bandwagon. I really didn't spend a lot of time on the internet except to check my email or do some occasional shopping.

One morning while Jaren was at preschool and Lynsi was sleeping, to kill some time, I jumped online to tie up some loose ends on his eBay auctions. Then I decided I would check my email, even though I rarely had anything super important. My emails were mostly ads or specials from various stores. But that day, I had received what I consider to be one of the most important emails of my life.

That day, September 22, I had an email from Scott McGrath. My stomach lurched as I saw the name on my computer screen. It was definitely unexpected, but looking back, the most unexpected part was how much my life would change that day. I was really very surprised that he had emailed me. True, I had sent him that card and even extended an invitation to visit if he wanted. I had included my email address, but I never really thought he would take me up on it. Many people had told me to let them know if they could do anything or if I needed anything, and I would of course thank them and did appreciate the offer, but I never did actually take them up on it. So you can imagine my surprise when this man, whom I did not even know, was taking me up on my offer and reached out to me.

The title of his email was "With Sympathy Too!" and this is what he wrote:

Lisa,

Thank you for the card. I am responding right away by email while this is still fresh in my head. I hope it reaches you, if not there is a "Thank you" card coming. My heart breaks for you and your children too. This pain is so unbelievable. And yes, like you know "Only you really know how you feel ..."

Everything is so overwhelming, but when Linda told me you wanted to send something, I felt so blessed. See, I learned about you not much earlier than when I started down this path. Cari and I had been visiting the night of August 13th. I was working on some proposals on the couch and she walked into the living room and told me about the accident. She had read about it in a later issue of the Hill City Times. She was shocked. That was the last real conversation I remember having with her. I was not feeling well that night and remember staying up kind of late with her watching the Olympics, before dozing off in bed, but do not remember visiting about really anything. Life becomes too routine. That has been stuck in my head ever since I found her on our bathroom floor struggling for life that next morning.

Even though we have not met yet, we belong to a club that neither one of us ever wanted to become members of. I offer to you the same invitation, to call me whenever you need to. I know I will get in touch with you soon ... I read your card twice and each time I read it, I cried even harder.

To let you know, the check you sent will be donated in Cari's name to Breast Cancer Research. She had a cousin die last November battling the disease. Cari was very passionate about raising funds for charities that fight for a cure. It only feels right, and if Jason was passionate about something, please let me know. I want to send you and your family the same gift.

Thank you!
Your New Friend,
Scott McGrath

As I read his message, tears streamed down my face. It was hard to believe that either one of us was going through this horrible situation. It was just not fair! Some days I felt as though maybe I was about ready to accept it, and although I didn't understand, I was trying to trust God's plan. But then other days, and this was one of them, I did not understand at all. How could something like this happen to such young people with young families? Anger, sadness, hopelessness, and disappointment, among other feelings, were all common emotions for me. *But* on this day, at least, I did not feel so alone. I felt I had someone I could talk to who knew exactly what I was going through. Yes, I had plenty of family members and close friends who were happy to listen or do anything for me, but it just was not the same.

I instantly responded.

Scott,

Thank you so much for responding. I am glad you received my card. I read it over and over again before I was sure I could send it. I was afraid it didn't sound as comforting as I meant it to, but I have learned that "comforting words" aren't always that comforting. I know our situations are a bit different, but they are ultimately the same—we have both lost our spouse and are single parents and it is hard to understand why.

I did meet Cari once, at Linda's wedding. I didn't remember her at first, but Linda sent me a picture and I instantly remembered her pretty smile! She seemed like a very sweet and caring person.

How are your kids doing? How old are they again? My son Jaren is 4 and in preschool. Our little baby girl, Lynsi, was born September 10. Jaren is doing well. He seems to understand everything fairly well. He knows that Daddy went to heaven to live with God and Jesus and that he is an angel now. I know he misses him and I hate that he was in the accident with us because he talks about it quite a bit and is afraid to travel and afraid of hitting a deer again. I don't blame him, I feel the same way. He is in preschool and seems to be doing very well. I don't know if he talks about it there or not. I know they learned about "family" a few weeks ago, but I don't know exactly what they talked about. It just breaks my heart when I hear him tell his little friends that he doesn't have a daddy anymore.

I have really been struggling since the baby was born. I think the whole postpartum emotional "stuff" with everything else added on has really taken a toll on me. I am just sooo sad that Jason is not here and I miss him sooo much. We have a brand-new baby and he is supposed to be here—we are supposed to be doing this together. We were so looking forward to her birth. We tried a couple years just to have her and now this. She is a very good baby and is doing well. I just can't believe she is going to grow up never physically knowing her daddy. It is just not fair and I will never understand it.

Did you know Jason at all? What a guy! Of course, looking back, I didn't really appreciate who he really was and how wonderful he really was until he was gone. We really take our lives and loved ones for granted sometimes, I think. I am like you—I really can't remember our last conversation. We were on our way home to Scott City from Healy from my baby shower. Jason and Jaren had spent the evening with my dad and had gone to the swimming pool. We met up at the swimming pool after the shower. I just really can't remember anything we talked about on the way home. That whole accident was a nightmare though, so I am not surprised I don't remember anything before it happened. I replay the accident in my head constantly and I just feel horrible for Jason. It really is a miracle that Jaren and I weren't hurt, but it doesn't change the fact that Jason lost his life.

I am sorry if I am rambling on and on, but for some reason it is making me feel better.

I am very glad that you are donating the memorial to Breast Cancer Research. I am an x-ray tech and I do mammograms, so I am very involved in breast cancer awareness, etc., etc. I feel very passionately toward the cause as well.

It was so hard to decide on a memorial. Jason loved golf and the Denver Broncos, but neither one of those really fit! I decided that the most important thing to him would be his kids, so we just set up a Kanak Children Education Fund. It has just been amazing and overwhelming how generous people are. Between you and me, as grateful as I am, I am kind of getting worn out writing thank-yous! I am estimating that we have sent close to 500. On top of that, I have had a lot of baby thank-yous to send too.

Well, I have probably gone on long enough. I know of a couple people who have lost a spouse, but haven't really felt comfortable talking to them. It almost seems easier to talk to someone I don't really know—especially since we are basically going through this at the same time. Everyone I have talked to went through it many years ago. I did have a lady from Salina send me a card who went through a similar situation a few years ago. She sent me her email address and I just haven't taken the time to email her. She doesn't even know me; she just must have read about it in the paper and wanted to reach out to me since she has been in this situation. I really need to email her and let her know how much I appreciate her contacting me.

Like, I said, Thank you for contacting me. I was hoping you would. I know we have to try and be strong for our kids but I have had days lately that I really didn't know if I could go on hurting this badly. Just writing this email, though, has helped because I know I am talking to someone who knows what I am going through. Thanks again and hopefully we can stay in touch and help encourage each other.

Lisa

After only receiving and then sending just one email, I already felt much better. I think there was a lot that I was holding inside for a variety of reasons. For one, I guess I felt like I didn't want to bother anyone with my problems or feelings. Second, I may have had a little tiny chip on my shoulder thinking that no one would understand so why make the effort to try and explain it to anyone? Maybe it was just easier talking to a stranger.

I had actually started counseling sessions with Pastor Dennis, and that did really seem to help. Seeking Christian-based counseling was very important to me. I needed to try and live through this and process it using my faith to the best of my ability. I knew I had to hold on to it no matter what. I can't exactly explain why I felt this way; I just did. I know that situations like this often result in people turning away from God and their faith, but I guess I look at it on the contrary. I believe that in situations like this God desires for us to draw closer to Him and to lean on Him even more for comfort, strength, and guidance. I can honestly say that I do not know how people without faith cope in situations like these.

Anyway, on a certain level, Dennis could also relate to my situation, and I also feel that was helpful as well. His first marriage had also ended, not by death but by divorce, but his current wife Betty had lost her first husband, so he had traveled the road right alongside her as a friend. Both Dennis and Betty were great to talk to and helped me a great deal.

After I replied to Scott's email, I must have checked every hour for the rest of the day to see if he had responded. Although he did not respond that day, I was excited to receive another email from him the next morning.

Chapter 20

Getting to Know Each Other

September 23, 2008

Lisa,

The card was very comforting, probably because I know the person on the other end has similar feelings. I don't know about you, but I am not sleeping very well. That is why I am up and emailing you at 4:45 a.m. Life for us has changed so much and the people that have reached out to help have been amazing, but it feels right to talk to you because we have just started down this road at similar times. Nobody's routine has totally changed like ours, or even yours. I cannot imagine having a child so shortly after losing a spouse. Even our situations are different, but I have found comfort in talking about my situation. The problem is finding someone who is comfortable talking about it with you and truly listening. I have started seeing a counselor with the children. She is a "Play Therapist" too and highly recommended. Plus with the age of Lilian, a grant was available. Do you see anyone?

Cari was an amazing person. I am having such a hard time letting go. That smile of hers is the hardest thing to imagine not seeing without looking at it in a picture. Plus talking to her about my day or hers. This pain is so unreal.

Our children seem to be handling it the best they can. Benton is 7 and has just started the second grade. He is our sensitive one and has really just shut down. He does not like to talk about Cari being gone very much. Lilian just turned 3 while Cari was in the hospital. I am sure that she and Jaren are kind of in the same mind-set. Lilian has in her mind right now though that we go to the hospital when we are sick and we do not come home, we go to heaven. It upsets me too when the kids talk about their mommy being gone also. Sometimes I think they are doing it at inappropriate times, but I know that is the only way they know how to deal with it.

I did not know Jason. I have seen a picture of him on Linda's MySpace page though. Yours and Linda's babies have very close birthdays, don't they? I have always enjoyed Linda from the first time I met her while Cari and I were dating in college. It was horrible hearing about the accident that night knowing Linda, but then thinking about you being pregnant at the time and your son being with you all. I cannot even imagine; the only thing I know is that it is a nightmare. Sitting by Cari's side for 15 days watching her being taken away from me was scary enough. Now I question every decision I had to make. I wonder how I will explain it to my children while they are growing up.

I know we have a long road ahead of us. When I first got back to Hays, people mentioned getting into certain men's groups around town to talk to others that have lost a wife. I thought they might be ok, but not right away. That is why I started to see someone one on one, but mostly for the children, so I know how to deal with them. I try to imagine what Cari would have done, how strong would she have been, would she feel as weak as I do, would she hurt as much as I do? These are all questions I will never have answers for, I just need to remember how much she loved me and realize I have a job to finish for her and me. It is sad I will not be going down this road with her, but I know she would want me to take care of our children and teach them what we believed life was all about. I know it is hard to want to go on carrying this pain, but I think about if there is life after this one and we get to be back with our loved ones, then I am not going to show up disappointing her. Because I believe I was never that way before or she would have never loved me as much as she did.

Well, do not ever feel like you are wasting my time with an email or a phone call …. I am always here. Thank you for reaching out; I might never have, and I have a hard time asking for help. So please feel free to contact me anytime.

Scott

As much as I wanted to be able to respond right away, taking care of a baby was a bit demanding and needed to be a priority. But at least I knew I had something to look forward to. I know I won't be able to share every email we exchanged, but I love sharing these first few because they really tell a lot about both our stories and lives during this time. Plus, looking back and trying to recall events during that time has proven to be a bit difficult. I think because of the trauma as well as having a baby and all the stress, I repressed a lot of memories. So the emails really help tell the story. When I finally had a few minutes, I continued our conversation with this:

September 24, 2008

Hello,

Well, it's been "one of those days" for me today. The baby didn't sleep very well last night, so I didn't get much sleep, so today has been pretty emotional for me. I just don't have any energy or desire to do anything. All I can do is cry. All I really want to do is sleep, especially since I don't think about everything when I am asleep. So I do know about the whole not being able to sleep thing. I couldn't sleep after the accident, so my doctor started me on Ambien, a sleeping medicine. It really helped during the last few weeks of the pregnancy. Now that the baby is here and I am nursing her, I can't take the medicine anymore. I have been taking Tylenol with codeine instead. It almost makes me too sleepy though. I think I am going to try going without and see how I do.

Having a new baby has been very hard. It is something that Jason and I were so excited about and supposed to be experiencing together. This may sound bad and I feel a little guilty about it, but I just don't feel all that happy to have a new baby. She is a precious little miracle, and a part of Jason, but like I said, without him here, it is just not as happy for me. I hope I get over that soon. Plus, since it has been over 4 years since I had a baby, I am still a little apprehensive about having a new baby again.

I am glad you are seeing a counselor with your kids. I am seeing my pastor for now. My doctor says if I keep having a hard time that he wants me to see a counselor and possibly psychiatrist. For right now, I am most comfortable seeing the pastor and trying to lean on faith to get me through. We think Jaren is doing well, so I haven't had him see anyone yet. There is an early childhood specialist that is kind of keeping an eye on him at school, but she says he is doing very well. I wonder if it won't hit him harder when he gets older. I know what you mean about the kids talking about it, but you are right, they need to talk about it. I know it is hard for you to hear them talk about it, as it is hard for me too for Jaren to talk about not having a daddy.

I am so sorry for what you had to go through with Cari being in the hospital on life support. I am sure you were faced with a million decisions to make and I am sure it is normal for you to question yourself. I am just trying to hold strong to the thought that they are in heaven and that it is the most amazing place and that they are now our guardian angels and we will be reunited one day.

I have had the same thought as you—what if the tables were turned and Jason was the one here still?

Right afterward, I wanted to trade places. I thought that he would be able to handle it much better than I am. At first, the overwhelming thing was that Jason paid all the bills and dealt with all the finances so I was clueless. Plus, I didn't even know for sure if he had life insurance. We didn't have wills or anything like that. You just don't think that it is something you should have to worry about at such a young age. I am feeling more comfortable with all that stuff now. It is like you said, it is just seeing them every day and talking about your day or whatever. Now, the hard part is just trying to get on with our lives. I know we have to be strong for the kids, but it is so hard and like you said, the pain is so unreal.

So, you are back in Hays? Are you working and are the kids in school? I had planned on taking 12 weeks off for maternity, but I may have to go back to work, just to take my mind off things and be around people. I am trying to get out and see people, but whenever I get together with friends, all I do is think about how they still have their husbands and their kids still have their fathers. Do you have family in Hays, or anyone helping you out? My mom has basically been staying with me since the accident. I dread when she decides not to. My parents live in Healy, which is only 24 miles away, and my mom works here in Scott City 3 days a week, but I am sure she misses being home with my dad. I just do not want to be alone. The thought makes me sick to my stomach.

I am really glad that we are talking. It is already helping me to talk to someone who is going through the same thing so thanks again for contacting me.

I hope you feel the same and hope you are feeling comfortable talking to me. I am praying for you and your kids. I just pray that God will help take some of the hurt away so that we can go on. I agree with you that they would want us to keep going on and take care of the kids and ourselves.

Talk to you later,
Lisa

September 25, 2008

Hi Lisa,

I know what you are talking about when you say "one of those days". I felt that way yesterday. Lilian (3) did finally sleep in her own bed last night and I was able to get a little more sleep. We all got around kind of normally this morning. I guess as normal as you can be. One thing I have noticed lately is not to put too much of a load on yourself …. Maybe women are different than men, but the stress of doing the everyday work and coming home and dealing with the kids alone has been hard. I am not one to ask for much help. I have a business here in Hays that I run basically by myself. Then I go home and deal with all that too. I have noticed that I need to start taking people up on the offers to help. I think I am going to send Lilian to my parents (Beloit) to watch her for a while. I need to reconnect with Benton (7). He has started the second grade and is doing pretty well, but is needing a lot more of my time than I am used to. Somedays I am really short-tempered with him and I don't want him to think I can't take care of him and Lilian. I did a bad thing and got right back into the grind of it all, work, school, family, and now it has taken a toll on me.

I am glad your family is close by and can be with you. Cari and I kind of liked being a little distant. We tried living in Beloit for a couple of years, but neither one of us liked it. Hays was always home to us. Because of me in business for myself and all the traveling around I always prepared for Cari to have to deal with the possibility of me being gone. So I had life insurance for the both of us, but also trusted the family business to her so she never had to worry about my paycheck leaving. It sounds like you have a lot of support, and that is great. I feel like I do too. I could not imagine going through this without anyone wanting to help. Just by reading into your emails, I can tell that you are blessed with a lot of family and friends that really want to help. I feel blessed that I am getting to know you as well. I wish this was not how our paths would have crossed, but we will make it.

Take care and talk to you later.

Scott

September 25, 2008

Scott,

Today, so far, has been much better. I put the baby in her crib in her room last night so that I didn't hear her every move and we slept much better.

You are right about not putting too much of a load on yourself. If something around the house doesn't get done, oh well. You have to make your kids and you a priority right now. I actually went back to work before I had the baby for a few weeks and it helped me. I am the supervisor of the radiology department here in Scott City, but I don't have near as much responsibility as running my own business so I can imagine you have a lot on your plate. Don't you think getting the kids back in somewhat of a "routine" is good though? That is what I have tried with Jaren. Since the baby came, he has been going to daycare in the morning and then either I or my mom take him to preschool from 12 to 3 p.m. I pick him up at 3:00 and then we come home and go from there. I have been trying to get out and do things and see people to pass the time. I still expect Jason to come home after 5:00. Jason was an accountant. He worked here in town at a small firm called Brass Tax. It was just him, his boss (the owner), and their secretary. He LOVED that job. It is the first job he had since we had been together that I could tell he really enjoyed. He was such a different person after going to work there. His boss loved him like a son too, so it has been super hard on him as well. They had a lot in common, mostly their love/obsession with golf.

Did you know we lived in Hays? We both went to school and met there. Jason worked at Brungardt, Hower, and I worked at the hospital. We lived there until July 2005 and moved to Scott City. I grew up in Healy, so it was basically a move closer to home. We really liked Hays; it was a great place to live. We were really happy in Scott City also.

I think I pretty much have all our financial issues figured out, but boy was that overwhelming on top of losing your husband and being 9 months pregnant. I had life insurance on him through my job as well as an Aflac accident policy. I have received both of those. Jason did have life insurance—he had just taken it out in November 2007. He had always had it through his work, but when he took this job in Scott City, there really wasn't much of a benefit package since it was an independently owned business. I had been on him for quite some time that we both needed to look into life insurance, but I didn't know he had gotten his. I do kind of remember him coming home one day and saying, "Well, I bought life insurance today," but we didn't really discuss it and I had to go through tons of files and piles of paperwork to find it. Jason took care of filing all our "important" papers too, and his filing system was not so good! Who knows when I will receive the life insurance, though? I have had to fill out a ton of paperwork. So, far, they are the only people that have made me cry on the phone!

Is it hard for you to talk to Cari's family or see them right now? I have had a hard time being around Jason's family just because it makes me think so much of him and how he was always around when his family was. I hope you have a good relationship with your in-laws.

I really admire you for doing it on your own right now! I am so afraid to be alone at home with both kids. Of course, I am new to the whole having 2 kids thing and having a new baby, so that is part of it. Don't be afraid to ask for help! I am not good at it either, but it is better than having things get out of control, especially emotionally.

I told you about the gal from Salina that contacted me, didn't I? If not, tell me, but she emailed me back and you will not believe what has happened to her. She lost her first husband when a car hit a deer and the deer flew into the windshield of his truck a few years ago. She since remarried. On August 8, after she had sent me the card, she and her family were involved in a head-on collision on the interstate and her second husband was killed. She and the kids were not hurt. Can you believe that? I did not even know what to say to her. I feel so bad for her. I can't imagine having to go through it all over again. She moved back home from Salina to Clay Center so that she could be around family. I just CAN NOT understand why this stuff has to happen. It is so not fair.

I am so appreciating our "discussions." It is really helping me and I hope it helps you too. I just think we can really relate to each other right now with what we are going through. Hope you had a good day.

Lisa

Having these discussions with Scott had inspired me to finally email that sweet lady from Salina who had reached out to me. I was devastated for her when she told me that her second husband had passed away not long after she had sent me that card. I felt really bad for her, and it also just instilled more fear in me than I already had. Not that I was anywhere close to being in another relationship; the reality was that I was very young, my kids were young, and I enjoyed being married and having a traditional family. I did not want to be alone the rest of my life, so I truly had hope that someday God would place the right man in my life. But now I just didn't know if I could ever open my heart and have to constantly worry about something like this happening again. I decided not to worry about it and to focus on my kids and the healing that I still needed to do.

I was having good days and bad days, along with some really, really bad days. I definitely think I was suffering from postpartum depression, on top of regular depression mixed in with post-traumatic stress disorder. But amid all that, I had made a new friend, and our "conversations" really gave me something to look forward to now. Plus, he really had a way with words. He gave me advice, encouragement, and insight into things that might not have occurred to me otherwise. And it was kind of fun getting to know someone new. I really missed having a companion to talk to, and although it sounds weird, in a way, I felt as though I was talking to Jason again.

Chapter 21

I Feel the Same Way

September 26, 2008

Hi Lisa,

Well, yesterday was not too bad. I am so relieved to know that you and Jason had that life insurance. You never wanted to know how it all works, but a little relief is there when you know that financially you may be ok. That is where I am at right now. It took forever to get death certificates.

I am glad that the children and you are sleeping better. I know that routine when you sleep lightly just so you are there when needed. I love being a dad because of that. I usually was up right away .... I can remember some nights though lying there waiting to see which one would get up first, pretending I was asleep. The things we do. I do believe the "routine" is a good thing. The kids seem to handle it very well.

Passing the time is all I try to do. So far I have not been able to stay a weekend in Hays. This weekend a friend and I are going to Manhattan to a KSU game. He is excited; he has been there for me since day one. He and his wife live in KC and he sat with me the whole time. He even sat with Cari when I had to come back to Hays for a day. Some people do amazing things for others in their time of need. I will probably never know how to pay him back ....
He has been there for me every step of the way.

I do enjoy visiting with you. I don't know if you do this though, but when typing emails you can start on a subject and just start going on like you are talking to Jason, and in my case Cari. I spend almost as much time deleting as typing. It helps me though. I really feel like I am making the choices Cari would have made. I always say that I wish I knew what Cari would do if she was in my shoes, but I loved her so much that I would not have wanted her to go through this either. It is not that I am a stronger person. I just never liked to see her unhappy.

As for the story about the lady in Salina, I remember you telling me about someone contacting you, but did not know her story. Let me tell you something about me that I do enjoy: I like to know someone's story. We all have one. When I visit with a person I love it when they tell me their story. People do it to me a lot; Cari was always amazed about that. She always would get a little upset when I would just start visiting sometimes, even with a stranger. I believe you can really know someone when they tell you their story. She sounds like an amazingly strong woman, to have contacted you after all that. I know, because if you would have not contacted me first, I would have never sought out to know your story ....

I do believe there are angels among us. It is just how deep we look into their souls. Each one of them has something to teach us, even if we never wanted them too. Thank you for being one.

I hope your weekend is good.

Scott

September 26, 2008

Hello,

Honestly, I hope I am not smothering you with these emails—please tell me if I am. It is just so weird how we both feel the same about so many things. Just like you said and I almost mentioned yesterday, I sort of feel as if I am talking to Jason as I write these emails.

Something else I have picked up on that we have in common is how much we love and cherish our spouses. I can tell how much you loved Carl just by your emails. You talk so highly of her and I think it is wonderful. I have done nothing but praise the person Jason was since he has been gone. I am just so proud of him. Isn't it sad that something like this had to happen for me to have all these feelings about him? I feel bad that I never really told him these things when he was alive. I really did take him for granted sometimes and did not give him the credit he deserved. He is the best thing that ever happened to me.

I found a picture frame at a store here in town and it says "The Best Thing I Have Done Was to Love This Man". The store owner and I both just cried when I bought it. I put a picture of me and him in it. He could really annoy me at times, but I would give ANYTHING to have him back right now. I just miss him so much. He was so good to me. I had been in some bad relationships in my life, so when I met Jason, I really thought he was too good to be true.

We really complemented each other too. Until this happened, I did not realize how many of our friends looked at us as such a great couple until they started telling me. He never got mad at me or yelled at me, no matter how mean I might have been to him. He never held a grudge or gave me the silent treatment. He constantly showered me with complements about everything—my clothes, the house, what I cooked. He did all the driving because he knew I hated to drive. I could have gone to that shower in Healy by myself, but he insisted on driving me over there. I wish now he hadn't.

We had our disagreements—mostly about golf. He golfed a lot more that I wish he would have. I always wanted him to spend more time with us, but he did golf in a lot of tournaments. He had really started to back off on the golf a bit though, knowing we were going to have two kids. We had also started going to a couples group through our church and we had really enjoyed that. In just the two or three sessions we were able to attend, we opened up so much to each other and we thought it was really going to make our marriage stronger.

Well, that's probably enough about that. It just makes me feel better to talk about him sometimes so thanks for listening.

I know what you mean about having friends that you don't know how you can ever thank. I have a ton of friends who have been here for me and I wish I knew a way to thank them. We have two sets of neighbors who we really bonded with last summer and spent a lot of time with. We all even went to Vegas last November and had a blast. They have been so good to me. The guys have been taking care of my yard every week. They are all so worried about me. They are great people and I am so blessed to have all my friends and family in my life.

Well, I hear the baby, so I better wrap up for now. I can't tell you how much this is helping me. Don't feel obligated to return each and every email if you don't want to or don't have time; I will understand. Don't think I am crazy, but I have been checking Jason's email since he has been gone and I have actually considered "emailing" him a time or two, just to write my thoughts down and feel like I am talking to him. I go to the cemetery and "talk" to him or talk to him in my prayers sometimes. I probably won't ever do it, but my point is that writing these thoughts in an email has been a big help.

Have a great time at the game and a safe trip. I have some friends from Hays coming to visit tomorrow, so I am looking forward to that.

Have a great weekend.

Lisa

It was amazing to me how we just seemed to be on the same page almost all the time. Some days he would write something that I was thinking or vice versa. And even if he did get annoyed by my emails, I don't think he would have ever admitted it. I could tell that it was really helping him as well. I often would think about what Jason would have done if things had been the other way around and he had lost me. To be honest, I can't even imagine it. I guess maybe that's why it didn't happen that way.

So far Scott and I had emailed each other every day for four days, and then the weekend came and I didn't hear from him again until the next Monday. It felt like experiencing withdrawal. How pathetic is that? I would check my email a couple times a day and then be disappointed when I had not received anything. Of course, then I became like an insecure teenager and started to tell myself that he was probably getting annoyed with me and was avoiding the situation.

Some days I really hate my mind and the way it works. For some reason I often think the worst. I guess I have this superstition that if I can think the worst, then it won't happen, if that even makes sense. I am also great—and by great I mean horrible—at "what ifs." I don't know why I have to question everything and oftentimes negatively. I honestly think a lot of it stems from the tragedy I had just experienced. So often we go through life hearing of situations but still thinking nothing like that could ever happen to us. But it was clear now that I am not resilient from these bad things, and if one bad thing could happen then what else could I be in for?

As much as I pleaded with God to take these thoughts away from me, I still continue to have them. But at least now I have recognized that they are not from God. The negative thoughts and "what ifs" are from Satan, and when I feel one coming on, I instantly turn to God for protection.

Chapter 22

One Month, Two Months, Day by Day

Well guess what, finally a new email from Scott:

September 29, 2008

Hi,

Do not worry about the emails. I feel the same way. I believe it makes us feel a little better.

Today is a very hard day. It has been one month since I had to leave her bedside and give her one last kiss on her lips. Cari had a thing for lip gloss. Seriously I think an addiction. I put it on her every day after we removed the ventilator and still kissed her lips every time I was holding her hand. That is all I can think about this morning, was that last kiss. I did not think this morning would be so hard. It started last night with my chest tightening up and my hands shaking uncontrollably. I am back in a trance today where I cannot believe this is real. When I do come to, I just start crying. Things are getting so crazy. I am usually really good with all the pressure. Actually Cari always said my better days were when thing were a little crazy. I worked better under pressure I guess. This is too crazy.

Well, I hope your weekend was good. I went to the KSU game with my best friend and we had a good time. But the whole time all I could think about was the last time Cari and I went to a game last year. It is funny how much you do together in just 9 short years of knowing each other. And still it is not enough. Benton is our little brain in the family. He has always wanted to be a scientist since the day he could talk. He loves experiments and we always let him be as creative as possible. The other night he said he was going to make a time machine and we would go back to Mommy. God, I wish he would …. Man, today is hard.

Thank you for the talks.

Scott

I know what I had to go through. Yes, it was tragic and unexpected, but it was sudden, and it was over. I simply just cannot imagine what Scott had to go through with Cari being on life support. What a struggle that must have been, as well as a roller coaster of emotions. I continued to feel horrible for him and what he had to experience, but I was glad that I could be there for him. It gave me a new sense of purpose. I guess in a way I felt like being there for him and listening to him somewhat took my mind off myself and what I was going through. I do not like to be in the spotlight. I would much rather fly under the radar then get a lot of attention. Plus, I just like to help others. It's part of why I went into health care and loved my job. I get a great sense of accomplishment and joy from helping others and feeling like I make a difference.

I truly believe that getting to know Scott was part of God's plan for my healing and helping me put one foot in front of the other and go on. By being there for him and feeling like I was helping him, I was also helping myself!

September 29, 2008

Hey Scott,

I am so so sorry that you are having a hard day. I know all about that and I wish there were something I could do or say to make it better. We want to hold on to our memories, but they are what make this hardest some days.

Tomorrow will be two months since the accident and the day I lost Jason. I can't even believe the whirlwind my life has been the past two months. My doctor has me on medicine for depression and anxiety and I think it is really helping. I don't cry my eyes out every day anymore. I hate being on medicine, and I have always kind of had a mind-over-matter outlook on things, but this was just too much to handle by myself. I really am starting to feel better.

I had a good weekend. My friends from Hays came down Saturday, so that was fun. They stayed all afternoon. We went over to Healy Saturday night for a birthday party and just stayed at my parents' house. Jaren and I still cannot travel well at night. Jaren cries and screams that he is scared and I don't blame him.

Linda is coming to see us today, so I am excited to see her and her new baby. We haven't seen each other since the babies have been born so we are pretty excited. Jason's mom is coming tonight to stay the week with us because my parents are out of town till Sunday.

The baby is crying so I have to go for now. I hope your day gets better. Feel free to call anytime, if you ever feel like talking in person. It is easy for me to want to shut myself off from the world when I am having a hard day, but if I talk to a friend it often helps.

Take care,
Lisa

September 30, 2008

Lisa,

I know what you are saying about the whirlwind. I never know the next minute when a triggering event will occur that upsets me. I do not think it is wrong to take something, I guess I am having problems accepting that I may need to take something. I talked to a doctor, but when we were visiting over the phone I must have played it off like nothing was bothering me anymore. The salesman in me can always put on a different face. I need to stop doing that to myself and really ask for help.

I am glad that you and the kids had a good weekend. Actually, I look forward to the weekends, because the kids and I have gone and done something every weekend. Last weekend I bought them a tire swing that is cut out like a horse, and we put it up out at our farm. They played on that thing for hours. Between that and taking turns getting rides on the 4wheelers, it made the weekend pretty good for them.

Tell Linda hi. I am glad everything is going well for them. I cannot believe she is a mommy though. How we change as the years go on.

Well I guess I will try to go back to sleep for a little while. Yep, still having problems sleeping every once in a while. Well, I will talk to you later. And I will try to call sometime soon. Thank you for always being there.

Scott

September 30, 2008

Hi there,

I can't believe it has been two months since the accident. It is still as vivid in my mind as if it were yesterday. It is good to have Linda and her mom here. Linda makes a lot of the same facial expressions as Jason, though, so I am really missing him. We have really good talks about Jason, though, and I think it makes us both feel better.

I know it's our kids that keep us going. If I didn't
have my kids to take care of, I don't know what I
would do. My problem is going to be getting up
the nerve to drive if I want to go somewhere on
the weekend. Jason drove everywhere. Besides that,
taking two kids somewhere by myself is a little scary
right now. I know I will eventually have to get over
that.

I hope you are having a better day today. One day at
a time, that is about all we can do.

Talk to you later,
Lisa

You are probably thinking at this point, "Is that all she did during this
time—sit around and send emails?" No, it wasn't all I did, but it was
definitely a highlight of my day and was actually very therapeutic.
At first, I wasn't even sure whether I wanted to share our emails in
this story. But once I went back and read through them, I felt they
really helped tell this part of our story quite well. I think it also gives
even more insight into our lives with Jason and Cari as well as the
amazing people they were.

Sometimes a few days would pass between responses and I might
have gotten a little impatient so I would go ahead and send another
email just to give me something to do to take my mind off whatever
I might have been faced with that day.

Chapter 23

A New Month

October 2, 2008

Hey Scott,

How are things going? I hope you and the kids are doing OK. We are doing OK here. Jason's mom is still here staying with us. Linda went home yesterday, which was hard for me. I really like being around her. We have really good talks. I feel close to Jason when I am with Linda. I guess she is the next best thing to him. I don't have any sisters either, so I am glad to have her. We have become much closer since Jason has been gone. I am trying to talk her into moving to Scott City, but I don't think I'll get it accomplished.

Do you have plans for the weekend? We don't have anything planned. Not sure how long Jason's mom is planning on staying, but I am sure not looking forward to being alone once she leaves. Maybe I can talk my mom into staying with me a while longer. Even when Jason was here, I never liked to stay alone at night. I just don't sleep well at all.

Gotta go for now. Let me know how you are doing.

Lisa

October 3, 2008

Hi,

We are doing OK too. The days are so different that each one is usually indescribable.

Cari never liked staying at the house either, even if she had the kids.

I guess our plans for the weekend are to go up to Beloit and get a computer desk for Ben's room. I have a spare computer in my office and he wants it in his room. They grow up really fast. This is usually the weekend we would go to the "Granny Mae's pumpkin patch" in Dorrance. We always had a blast, and the kids know we go every year. Last night when Cari's mom mentioned it I broke out into tears (like now), telling her I couldn't do it. I think they are going to take them.

Those things are so hard. I really loved our family outings. They always made me realize how blessed I really was.

Scott

October 3, 2008

Hey Scott,

Things sure are different without them, aren't they? I really do not look to forward the weekends, because, like you said, that is when we had family outings or did things together. Jason and I actually went down to Garden City quite frequently, just the two of us, and I really miss that too. I have been trying to do things around the house to keep me busy and I have been trying to get out of the house more. It's almost like I am getting tired of being home, waiting for Jason to come home and he doesn't. He was gone golfing a lot of weekends during the summer, but this was the time of year that he was home most weekends and we could do things together.

I have had family start talking about holiday plans already and I have to tell them that I am basically living day by day right now and that I cannot even think about the holidays. I am really dreading November. Our anniversary is November 17 and my birthday is November 24, plus Thanksgiving .... We, especially Jason, always made our anniversary and my birthday special. We usually went out of town somewhere to celebrate. Plus, Jason really liked to buy people presents, so he always spoiled me on our anniversary, my birthday, and holidays. It was really nice that he was that way, unnecessary, but nice. He loved Christmas too. He was the super shopper and always went crazy buying our family gifts. He even kept a spreadsheet. I just can't believe he won't be here. I just don't even want to think about it.

Well, I don't know much else tonight. I hope you have a good weekend.

Talk to you later,
Lisa

October 5, 2008

Hi Lisa,

Yes, things are very different …. I am having a hard time with the holiday plans too. My birthday is October 29th. Not only is it my birthday but will be 2 months since Cari's death. Her birthday is November 19th. We were supposed to have a big celebration in Denver the weekend of the 15th. My grandmother lives there and it is her 80th birthday. It was to be Cari's 30th. This is just all wrong.

Christmas will be my hardest one. I proposed to Cari on Christmas day in 2000. After that, every Christmas I bought her a piece of jewelry that would represent each Christmas we were together, and it was always diamonds. She never really could stand surprises, so she could expect that I was going to get her a piece of jewelry that would have diamonds. A diamond for every Christmas I spent with her. This was going to be 8. These next few months are going to be our hardest I am sure. Like you said, "One day at a time." I guess we will spoil our kids.

Our weekend was ok. Both kids went to Cari's parents for the weekend. They went to a pumpkin patch and had a good time. All I did was spent the whole time riding Cari's four-wheeler around our farm and in the country. I went everywhere on it. Those things are starting to become very hard to hold onto.

I hope you had a good weekend. It was kind of peaceful to be alone, but at the same time very hard. And coming home is getting harder. I still expect Cari to be here when we get home or calling me to see when we will be getting home. I usually go out and stay at our farm a lot during this time of the year, to hunt, work with our dog, or just enjoy the cooler fall days working outdoors.

Well, Lili is needing my attention, so I guess I better go. Talk to you later.

Scott

Therapy is no joke. Granted, there a lot of jokes about therapy, and in fact Jason used to joke that my shopping "addiction" (particularly shoes) was probably still cheaper than therapy. But that is beside the point. Seriously, as humans we theoretically don't have a problem with trying to better or take care of our physical body through diet and exercise. Isn't our mental and emotional health just as important? Yet there seems to be a strong stigma about seeking therapy when it comes to these aspects. I guess maybe people are embarrassed by it or feel weak.

I can see, however, that at this stage of my life I needed all the help I could get with my mental and emotional health. I did have regular sessions with my pastor, and he was amazing. I truly feel some of the best therapy comes from talking with someone who can relate on some level with what you are going through.

Pastor Dennis was definitely a godsend for a lot of reasons, but one specific insight that I will always remember and often share with others to this day is this: You can't change people, but you can pray for them, and you can pray for yourself to accept them for who or what they are. At the time, I was obviously very sensitive about a lot of issues and felt overwhelmed by various people in my life. I would share my frustrations with him. It really changed my outlook the day he shared this insight with me.

As much as I appreciated and definitely benefited from my sessions with Pastor Dennis, the best therapy of all was really in my "discussions" with Scott. As I already mentioned, feeling I was helping him was really helping me just as much. I really looked forward to his emails and felt very comfortable sharing anything and everything with him. And I believe that he felt the same way and also felt as if he had a new purpose in being there for me as well.

After two and a half months of only knowing Scott through emails and an occasional phone conversation, I knew I wanted to meet this man and his children in person. Luckily, the feeling was mutual, because in this email, he offered to come to Scott City on his way home from a trip to Denver:

> Hi Lisa,
>
> I was just thinking about you last night when my kids were flying around like screaming banshees and I was trying to get them ready for bed. At least you only have one that moves around a lot. Sometimes I wonder what is in that candy they get at Halloween time. I hope everything is going ok ….
>
> I think about you all a lot, just because I am getting a little tired of the sympathy from others that really do not understand. Many people will tell me to send my kids over to play anytime when I just wish they would say. "Let me take your kids to play with my

kids and give you a little time to clean or grocery shop or just have a little time to yourself" …. They should know that I am not going to call and say, "Come pick up my kids please!" Maybe I am just going crazy ….

You are the only one that I feel I can really talk to. I hope that is ok. Every time I talk to someone else I feel like I am on show. Some are comfortable and some are not. I was thinking that maybe the kids and I would try to swing by Scott City on our way to or from Denver next weekend. I thought I would see what your plans were. Maybe I could take you all out to dinner. We are going out there for my grandmother's 80th birthday. I was not going to go, but she is the only other member of my family that has lost a spouse. She flew to KC the day after Cari was in the hospital to be with me and I thought I probably owe it to her to be there. She has always been really close to me, but still I have not been able to talk to her about everything.

I am really trying to avoid work today …. Each day becomes more overwhelming …. I never used to look for the weekends to come so fast, but even those are becoming harder. My brother put his condo out in Keystone, Colorado up for sale. I told him if it had one more bedroom I would have sent him the cash yesterday and would have been moving today. I really am starting to hate Hays. I have no one here to talk to. None of our friends here have spoken to me since the funeral. Plus, the school can't seem to control Benton. They keep asking me if I have thought about medicating him, but our therapist says not to. This LIFE is crazy. I do not want it!

This is not what I signed up for, and I know you feel the same way.

Well, I have a mess to take care of today, and I know no one is going to do it for me, so I guess I better start working. Take care, let me know about next weekend if you are available.

Talk to you later.
Scott

Chapter 24

Nice to Finally Meet You!

It was now November, which is usually my favorite month of the year. My birthday is in November, and I have always loved my birthday, but also Jason and I were married in November. We would have celebrated our seventh anniversary that year. Aside from those reasons, I have always loved Thanksgiving too, simply because I love getting together with family and, of course, eating delicious food. However, this year, none of these things were exciting to me, and in fact, the thought of them was downright depressing.

I did, however, have something I was looking forward to, and that was meeting Scott and his kids. The plan was for them to come to Scott City on their way home from Denver on the afternoon of the sixteenth. I don't know why, but I was extremely nervous yet excited to meet them. Even though we had never met in person, I felt as if I had known him and been friends a really long time, just by exchanging emails and phone conversations for the past two months.

I nervously kept looking out the window in expectation of their arrival. When they finally arrived and that doorbell rang, I froze.

I had no idea what to do or say! Of course, I didn't have to open the door because Jaren beat me to it. There they stood. Excitement instantly filled the children, and they were off running, leaving Scott and me just awkwardly standing there. The only thing I could think of is how much I just wanted to hug him and tell him how sorry I was in person. But I knew that would be even more awkward, so we said our hellos and I invited him in.

It was probably good that we did have the kids there to distract us, because otherwise I am not sure that either of us would have known what to say. At first it was mostly chitchat and talking about the kids. I think at first we were both thinking that this seemed much easier through email. But once we got to talking, we realized we could talk for hours.

I could definitely tell that he was very outgoing and a salesman because he did most of the talking. I was fine with it, though, because I am actually a much better listener than talker. Either way, it was good for both of us to finally be able to talk in person to someone who, for the most part, knew exactly what life was feeling like. I don't think he had really talked much to anyone about Cari's condition and what had happened, so I think he needed to talk to someone about it.

As he told me about her condition as well as the series of events that took place up to her passing, I listened with disbelief. A year before, in July of 2007, she fainted at home in the bathroom one night as she was brushing her teeth. Scott happened to be right beside her and witnessed it. He caught her and lowered her to the floor. She had no pulse so he started chest compressions. He compressed one time and she woke up. She was very disoriented and did not feel well. Scott then took her to the ER in Hays that night. They admitted her for testing and diagnosed her with "neurocardiogenic syncope." He said they weren't exactly sure what was causing it, but that basically her heart rate and blood pressure would drop, leading to reduced blood flow to her brain, which caused her to pass out.

She saw a cardiologist who was hopeful it could be controlled with medication. She started taking the medication and did well until she experienced another fainting episode three months later, in October. She was attending a festival with some friends when she passed out. Luckily, there were two nurses close by, as she had to be resuscitated. She was again admitted to the hospital and underwent two days of testing. There were no new findings and still no explanation of what was causing the episodes. The cardiologist opted to change her medication dosage and see if that made a difference.

Five months later, in March 2008, she was at a restaurant with friends and fainted again. She did not need to be resuscitated this time, but she did fall and hit her head, requiring stitches and another hospital admission. At this point she and Scott had both become very frustrated with the situation and asked to be referred to another cardiologist at a larger facility.

She was referred to a cardiologist at KU Med who said he agreed with her diagnosis as well. He felt that her medications and dosages should be altered. She was feeling really good on the new medications, so Scott suggested they take a trip to Colorado to celebrate their anniversary, which was August 4. They went to Colorado, had a wonderful time, and she felt great. However, ten days later, on August 14, she experienced yet another episode.

That morning Cari seemed to be taking an unusually long time in the bathroom getting ready. Scott had just woken up the kids to get them ready for the day and needed to get himself ready. He knocked on the door, and there was no answer. He tried to open it but couldn't, because she was lying against it. Once he was finally able to get into the bathroom, she was unconscious and not breathing. He could tell that she had felt one of her episodes coming on, as her doctor had told her if she felt one, she should lie down and elevate her legs above her heart. He found her lying down with her legs on the edge of the bathtub.

He immediately called 911, and they instructed him to start CPR. Police officers were the first to arrive, and Benton opened the door for them. The officers then attended to Cari so Scott could try and calm the kids. He took them to a bedroom and tried to comfort them while the officers moved Cari to the living room and continued CPR. Once EMS arrived, they were able to revive her and get her to the hospital. They did tests on her there and the doctors expressed their concern that her brain may have been without oxygen too long but that they could fly her to Kansas City. Scott opted to do that and provide her with every possible chance of surviving this unimaginable situation.

Although I too had tragically lost my husband, it was quickly over and done, and there was never any false hope. As I heard Scott's story, I remember thinking that I absolutely could not imagine going through everything he went through, from finding her unconscious in the bathroom to her being airlifted to Kansas City and then put on life support.

At the time I found it absolutely ironic that the night before he found her unconscious in the bathroom was when he first heard about Jason's death and my situation. Cari had read or otherwise heard about it and told Scott that night that Linda's brother, Jason, had been killed in a car accident and left a four-year-old son and eight-months pregnant wife. Believe it or not, this news then prompted them to have a conversation about end-of-life choices and what each of them would want if something were to happen to either of them.

As he continued to share details of the experience, it greatly saddened me that he and his kids had had to endure it. He tried very hard to hide it, but I could sense a great deal of anger and frustration toward doctors, family members, and mostly himself. He was really searching to place blame and seemed to be blaming himself and second-guessing his every decision. He shared with me that he had not been and was not in a very good place with his faith and was also very angry with God.

I honestly did not know how to respond to his feelings, as my situation was quite different. Sure, I was angry at times but not really at anyone specifically, just mostly at the situation. Who or what was I going to blame? The deer? The people in the car that hit it? At times I did feel that if I could find someone or something to blame, maybe that would justify the situation. Some days I even went so far as to blame myself and the pregnancy: if I had not been pregnant, then there would not have been a baby shower, and we would not have been on the road that night. Or if Jason had just stayed back and played golf instead of taking me, then it would not have happened either. But guess what, it did happen, and playing the blame game or being angry was not going to help anything. So very early on, I had accepted that it was a freak, tragic accident, and there was nothing anyone could have done.

But I could see that accepting the situation was not something that would come easily for Scott, and I could also totally empathize with him. Yes, at first there was a shred of hope that Jason would make it, since he still had a pulse when the ambulance took him away. But that hope was very short-lived as he passed away on the way to the hospital, and even though the doctors and staff did everything in their power to revive him, God had taken him pretty much instantly.

Now why this was different for Scott and Cari, I will never know, but for whatever reason, it was God's plan. Yes, they were able to revive her, and she did survive the transfer to Kansas City. Did the tests there look good? No. Were the machines keeping her alive? Yes. So this gave them hope, and as long as there is even the tiniest amount of hope, who wouldn't want to keep fighting and doing everything possible to bring a loved one back?

Cari spent almost two weeks at KU Med, and I cannot imagine what those two weeks were like for Scott and their families. To this day, I still do not know all the details, and I do not need to know.

Numerous doctors were consulted on her case, and a variety of tests and procedures were performed, but nothing seemed to be changing.

The next part of his story was completely heart-wrenching. Cari had been on life support for five days, and the time had come to make a decision on where to go with her care. Basically, their options were to keep her on life support indefinitely or remove it and see what happened. Can you imagine being faced with that decision? I sure couldn't, but Scott was. He told them that he needed the night to make his decision and needed to be with his children. They knew that this was coming, but at the time their main goal was to make it past Lilian's birthday, which was August 22. He said he will never forget having to celebrate her third birthday at a picnic spot just outside the hospital, especially when Cari had been preparing for it for weeks prior to the episode. But they celebrated it the best they could, considering the situation.

After hearing from the doctors that he needed to make this impossible decision, Scott felt that he just needed to be with his kids. He left the hospital and went to the family friend's house where they were staying. As he was giving Benton a bath and getting him ready for bed, Benton asked about his mommy. Scott decided that he needed to be completely honest with Benton, so he told his seven-year-old son that things did not look good for his mommy. He told him that most likely she would not be able to live without the machines. I can only imagine the devastation and disappointment that this poor little boy felt at that moment, considering how very close their relationship had been. He began crying and screaming that he wanted to see his mommy. Not knowing any other way to console him, Scott and his mom took the kids back to the hospital. He took Benton in her room alone and tried his best to explain the circumstances and how they needed to decide if they should keep her on the machines or not. With the maturity of a child well past his years, he looked at Scott and said, "Daddy, Mommy would not want to live like that." And that was when Scott knew his decision.

The next day, Scott informed the medical staff that he had decided to remove the life support. Since Cari was an organ donor, the first step was to meet with the organ donation consultants and assess which organs would be viable and eligible for donation. They already knew that her heart could not be donated, but Scott agreed to donate anything else except for her skin and tissue.

I had no idea how the organ donation process even worked, so I listened with astonishment as he then explained how it happened. They scheduled everything for 1:00 p.m. that day. For organs to be viable for donation, a patient must pass away within one hour of removing all life-sustaining measures. But Cari did not pass away within an hour, so her organs could not be donated. She didn't pass away that day even. She lived another ten days before passing on August 29.

I listened in disbelief as Scott told me everything he had been through. At this point, the kids had started to get a little rambunctious, so we decided we would go out in the backyard and let them run off some energy. As I stood out back with this man and our children, I felt overwhelmed with the reality of our situations. But as our moods were lightened by watching the kids laugh and play, I was also reminded of how thankful I truly was for those precious children.

If there is one thing I have learned about children through all of this, it is that they are resilient and matter-of-fact. As a parent you constantly worry about your kids and their well-being, so when they are faced with the loss of a loved one, especially a parent, you worry about how they will cope. And I did worry *a lot* about how this would all affect the kids. To read about the accident is just dealing with words on a page. My words to describe something that horrific are no comparison to living it. I had no idea what impact it would have on Jaren or what he would remember. Would he have nightmares? Would he have horrific fears of riding in a car or at night? And then of course at the time my biggest worry was that he would grow up without a father.

And what about Scott's kids? Their experience was devastating as well. Would they be scared of doctors or hospitals? Whenever someone got sick, would they worry they were going to die? Plus, aside from our worries, our friends and family constantly worried about our ability to cope with the grief and loss of our spouses and still be able to function enough to care for our children. There was just a whole lot of worrying going on!

But kids are simply accepting and don't seem to dwell on things the way adults do. Yes, they are sad, and when you bring up the situation, they may express their sadness, but they also just accept what happened and seem to try and move on to their next activity in life. I often say that I wish I had childlike faith. As an adult, I want to question everything, and I want an answer. I have a hard time trusting God's plan and seeing the reasons for it. Children just accept the situation for what it is. So as far as Benton, Lilian, and Jaren were concerned, their mom and dad went to live in heaven with God and Jesus. Period. And that was exactly what they told people. They didn't hash out the details; they didn't question why. They just accepted reality for what it was.

Still, it wasn't as if they just forgot about it instantly. They have had sad, difficult times, but those thoughts were often gone just as quickly as they popped into their heads. But what do we do as adults? We revisit a situation over and over and question over and over: *Why* did this happen? What could I have done differently? How could I have prevented this? Why, God? *Why?* I did this over and over. I still do this. But this situation also made me realize something. God's thoughts and plans are way beyond our interpretation, and no amount of questioning them will ever result in an answer, one that we are satisfied with, anyway.

At one point during this time, I was led to a passage in Isaiah that says,

> For my thoughts are not your thoughts,
> neither are your ways my ways ....
>
> As the heavens are higher than the earth,
> so are my ways higher than your ways
> and my thoughts than your thoughts (Isaiah 55:8–9)

My Bible has insights that often give an additional interpretation to the scriptures and this passage had one. It said, "The Creator needs no creature to interpret His way. His reasons. His style. His vantage point is infinity. It is too high. We cannot attain it. And so we accept rather than explain. We trust rather than try to make it all fit together so perfectly it squeaks." *We accept rather than explain.* Fast forward a couple years, and I was still having a hard time wanting answers for the situations we are faced with.

Then one Sunday the pastor at church preached on this exact topic, and for some reason her words finally sunk into me. "Hit me like a ton of bricks" might be a better description. She said these words: "There are things that happen in this life that I cannot explain, but with faith I accept it." I cried right then and there sitting in that pew. I was so overwhelmed with emotion that I just cried. It wasn't because I was sad, it was because the Holy Spirit just hit me over the head with the peace that passes understanding.

Chapter 25

Highs and Lows

That November afternoon spending time with Scott and his kids made for one of the best days I had had in what seemed like forever. Even though our reason for even meeting in the first place was tragic and devastating, little did we know God was hard at work in our lives. I think the anticipation of the meeting was probably the most nerve-racking, because the actual visit was wonderful and surprisingly comfortable. I truly hated to see them leave, but I felt that this would definitely not be a one-time meeting.

Despite having such a great day and going to bed that night with a renewed sense of strength and hope, the next morning I woke up feeling completely defeated and heartbroken. It was November 17 and would have been Jason's and my seventh wedding anniversary. The words *till death do us part* kept coming to mind, and I was unbearably sad. The entire situation kept playing over and over in my head, and I could make no sense of it.

My mom was supposed to come spend most of the day here and watch Lynsi, so that I could just do whatever I felt like, whether spending time alone or with her as company. She was only able to come until 10:00 a.m. because she got called to go to work. So I went out to the cemetery while she was here that morning. I hated that the weather was so beautiful that morning, because it reminded me even more of our wedding day. The weather was awesome—seventy degrees on November 17, 2001. Then the next day when we were leaving for Jamaica, the weather turned cold and dreary, so we were excited that we were going where the weather was nice. I wish it had just been cold and dreary to match how I was feeling, but it probably just would have made me feel even worse.

When I got back to my house, I had an email from Linda thanking me for loving her brother so much for the past seven years. I completely lost it and broke down crying. I just could not believe this was happening. This was not how my life was supposed to be. I needed something to take my mind off of it all. I had just recently joined Facebook, so I decided to jump on and see what was happening in the social world. In those days, whenever you first logged in to Facebook, at the top of the page the greeting said, "How are you feeling today?" Without even thinking much about it, my fingers typed "heartbroken" and hit enter.

I decided I didn't have the mental energy for Facebook that day, so I went back to check email again. This email from Scott was definitely a much-needed spirit lifter:

Hey there,

I wanted to let you know that the kids and I really enjoyed spending time with you all. Overall I think they got along pretty good. I know today may be hard, but you seem to be doing pretty well with everything, unless you were hiding a lot of your emotions like I was. I find it easier to push them down deeper the further I go. If you want to call me anytime today, I will be available …. I know I have not gone through the anniversary yet, but I feel like this birthday of Cari's is going to be very hard. I think I am going to buy the kids gifts to open …. Because without the birth of Cari, I would not be able to celebrate their lives, and even though I could have never imagined life without Cari; life without the kids is unthinkable.

Take care today and hope to visit again soon.

Scott

His words were such a great reminder to me of how thankful I truly was for my marriage, because without it I would not have my two beautiful children. I could have lost them both that day as well, but I didn't. I was grateful for Scott's email and the shift in perspective for my day. It also boosted my spirits to hear that they enjoyed our visit and hoped to visit again!

And it also made me shift the focus away from feeling sorry for myself and think about what he faced this week. Wednesday would have been Cari's thirtieth birthday, and I knew he was really dreading it. They had even planned a trip to Cancún for her birthday, and he was really looking forward to it since he had never been on a beach vacation before.

Ugh, this was so hard. Not to mention that all these special dates— Thanksgiving the next week and then Christmas in a month—made it even that much harder. But looking ahead in dread wasn't going to help anything, so I tried to concentrate on just getting through the day. Tomorrow would be a new day. And I did actually have something to look forward to. I was going on a weekend shopping trip with some of my good friends from Hays. They knew my birthday was coming up, and with everything I had been through, they wanted to do something for me.

Our shopping trips were always epic. We often joked that eventually we might have to consider renting a trailer, since we had already conquered the art of completely filling the back of the largest SUV any of us owned. We could definitely shop literally till we dropped, usually sometime around midnight. As much as I loved living in Scott City and being close to my family and friends there, I definitely missed my Hays friends and was looking forward to this girls' weekend with them.

My reminiscing was interrupted by the doorbell. *Ugh*, who could that be? I was definitely not in the mood to see anyone. I opened the door and was greeted by the lady from the flower shop. For a moment I felt excitement thinking about how Jason always sent me roses on our anniversary, but then that thought was crushed by the reality that they were not from him. Honestly—and I know it might sound very rude and ungrateful—I was sick of flowers. At that time, I associated flowers with a funeral, so what I really wanted to do was throw them out the door. But I didn't. I tried to let those flowers take me back to finding things to be grateful for instead of everything I felt that I had lost. I directed my thoughts back to the weekend and how much I was looking forward to getting out of town and seeing friends. I decided to send Scott a message and see if he would be around and interested in getting together.

After I finished messaging him, I noticed I had received a new message from a good friend. What a blessing that message was to me that day, as she sent me these two very encouraging verses that really helped me get through my day:

> For his anger lasts only a moment,
> but his favor lasts a lifetime;

weeping may remain for a night,
   but rejoicing comes in the morning. (Psalm 30: 5)

The Lord is close to the brokenhearted
   and saves those who are crushed in spirit.
(Psalm 34:18)

How true and comforting these verses were to me. As sad as I was, the day would soon be over, and tomorrow would be a new day. No matter what, the Lord would be there for me. The next day did in fact bring rejoicing for me, as Scott and I made plans to meet for breakfast Friday morning. It felt so good to have things to look forward to again.

As Friday approached, I started to have second thoughts about leaving town. This would be the first time I had left my kids since everything had happened. It would also be the farthest I had driven since the accident. Fear started to set in, and I started playing what-if scenarios over and over in my mind. Before the accident and my current situation, I don't ever remember being so fearful about so many things.

Now the fear was almost paralyzing to me. I felt I couldn't do it, and it would be selfish for me to go and leave my four-year-old and two-month-old in someone else's care. Luckily, I have a mother who can always make me feel better; she encouraged me to go ahead with my plans and do this for myself. I knew my kids were in great hands with her, and I knew that fear was from Satan. I determined not to let him steal an opportunity that would bring me joy after so many weeks of heartache.

Although it was only the second time I had seen Scott in person, it felt as if we had been friends forever. I think after the difficult week for both of us, it felt good to be able to meet in person. It sounds and felt really strange, but for some reason in the back of my mind it sort of felt like a date. But I knew that I couldn't think of it that way. It was way too soon, wasn't it? Still, something just felt different. Hopeful is a good word to describe how I was feeling, although I wasn't sure what I was hopeful for just yet.

The main focus of our conversation that morning over breakfast was Scott's experience that Wednesday on Cari's birthday. He had decided to drive to Beloit to visit her grave. Over the course of the last three months, he had driven to Beloit most weekends and Wednesdays just to visit her grave. He still felt as though he could be close to her in a sense. This Wednesday trip, though, proved to be very different. He spent a long time just lying in the grass next to her grave. He shared with me that many thoughts went through his mind like every other time— many questions, with lots of pain.

As he lay there that day he was drawn to the clouds. He watched the clouds and really noticed how he could make out different shapes. One in particular that day looked like a calla lily, which was Cari's favorite flower. Seeing that brought him an overwhelming sense of peace, almost as if she had sent him a message that everything would be OK. He told me that as he left the cemetery he felt as if she was telling him to let her go, that she was fine, and that he was going to be fine too. Knowing the type of person she was, he felt that she wouldn't want him living a sad story over and over every day. He too expressed that he had a newfound sense of hope and a renewed sense of purpose. We only have this one life to live, and we need to live it to the fullest.

I listened to him, thinking how glad I was that our paths had crossed. He was the only person who "got it," and he felt the same about me. I think I could have sat there talking to him all day, but there was shopping to be done. As we walked outside the restaurant, I had an overwhelming urge to hug him, so I asked if I could. *Oh, Lord, what did I just do?* Was he going to think it was awkward and I was weird? I was clearly overthinking, as it didn't even faze him. He just turned and hugged me, and it wasn't awkward or weird. It honestly just felt like two good friends being there for each other.

For some reason I felt giddy the rest of the day. It was confusing. My head kept telling me that it was crazy to think that this was or could be anything other than a friendship. It was way too soon to even consider anything else. But the feeling was growing that there could be something romantic between the two of us. I couldn't stop thinking about the situation. I talked to my friends about him a little bit over the weekend only because they knew I had planned to meet him for breakfast before we left, and they were just curious about him.

I found myself wondering what he was doing all weekend and wanting to text him. I didn't want to give him the wrong impression though. Regardless, I did text him a few times. The weekend with my friends was great, but I felt very awkward and sad at times when the girls talked about their husbands or families and upcoming holiday plans. Those subjects were all depressing to me, and I didn't even want to think about them.

It was good to get away, though I definitely missed my kids. Still, I dreaded going home. I have always loved my birthday, but this year I was not looking forward to it at all. Plus, it was Thanksgiving week, and I was dreading that the most. I was born on Thanksgiving Day, so my birthday is always close to or on it. It's amazing how one life-altering event can change your perspective on the things you normally love and enjoy. If I could have had my way, I would have preferred to just stay in my pajamas, watch the Macy's parade, go nowhere, see no one, and do nothing.

Yeah, I guess you could say I was feeling depressed. I have already mentioned it, but postpartum depression on top of losing a spouse depression, and post-traumatic event depression was a whole lot of depression to try and function with. Top that all with holiday anxiety and I was a hot mess. We normally alternated years spending Thanksgiving with our two families. The Kanaks always gathered at Grandma Bea and Grandpa Joe's house (Jason's grandparents), and Jason's mom was really hoping that I would come this year and bring the kids. Many of them had not seen Lynsi yet, so she thought it would be a great opportunity for them to see us all. I knew how hard it was going to be for all of them to celebrate the first holiday without Jason, so the sympathetic part of me really felt obligated. But the grieving widow part of me could hardly stomach the thought of traveling to my late husband's home town to spend Thanksgiving without him.

My side of the family had been invited to my aunt's house in Colby for Thanksgiving, so that was what my parents planned to do. My mom really wanted us to come with them. She did not want me to stay at home alone, as she was really worried about my depression. Plus, we did not see that side of the family very often, and she thought it would be good for me. She suggested that, if I preferred, they would then drive me to Atwood to see Jason's family. Her suggestion seemed much more doable than me trying to go alone with the kids.

As Thanksgiving Day approached, though, I felt so much anxiety and honestly was dreading it. But I think the anticipation of a situation can often be ten times worse than the actual situation turns out to be; that was the case here. I was worried that I would walk in the door and would feel an awkward sense of everyone feeling sorry for me. But it wasn't that way at all. It was simply good to see family that I hadn't seen in a long time, and no one even mentioned or made a big deal about anything. Most people were preoccupied with playing with the kids, so it was actually really nice.

But as we got in the car to head to Atwood, my feelings of anxiety and dread were back. I didn't know if I could do it. It's a good thing I wasn't driving; I probably would have just driven straight home. As we pulled into Atwood, I felt sick, and as we parked the car outside

Jason's cousin's house where everyone was meeting, I burst into tears. I had never been around any of Jason's family without him there too. I didn't think I could do it. It was going to be too hard. But then it dawned on me, this wasn't hard. I had been through lots of hard this past couple months and so far had survived, so seeing some wonderful people who loved me like part of their family should not be "hard."

Again, the anticipation was the worst part; the actual visit was wonderful. They all enjoyed getting to meet baby Lynsi, and of course Jaren had everyone in stitches, laughing at him and his Spiderman antics and maneuvers that day. Every once in a while, there would be an awkward silence, and we all just felt like something—or someone—was missing, but then Jaren would come flying off the stairwell and land in Spiderman crouch, and we would all be laughing again. Sometimes I think God uses kids to lighten the mood and the situation. Anyway, He definitely did that day, and I was so thankful. All in all, I was just super thankful to have survived the first Thanksgiving without Jason.

Even though I was surrounded by and preoccupied with family that day, I couldn't help wondering how Scott and his kids were doing and how their Thanksgiving was going. Scott and I had shared how much we were both dreading the holidays this year and seeing family. They, too, spent time with each other's families during holidays, and it would be vastly different this year without them. I had already learned that Scott preferred to be by himself to process things and grieve alone. Being around people made him uncomfortable, and he just felt awkward because most people, even friends and family, didn't really know what to say when they were around him. I, on the other hand, felt better when I was with people, whether friends or family. My mind and my thoughts were my worst enemy whenever I was alone, and all I would do was focus on how depressed I felt. So being with my family on Thanksgiving was really good for me.

After we got back home that Thanksgiving evening, my curiosity got the best of me, and I called Scott to check up on him and see how his day was. He and his kids had traveled back to his hometown of Beloit for the day. As I had suspected, Scott opted to go off alone and hunt most of the day. Being around his family was just way too much for him to handle. He then decided that he didn't even want to stay the entire weekend, so he left the kids with his parents and drove back to Hays that evening.

We chatted about my weekend and other small talk, which led to him telling me that he thought he might paint his living room. He and Cari had picked out paint but never got around to painting, and he wanted to make a change. He decided with the kids gone it would be a good time to do it. For some unknown reason (I say unknown because I really do not enjoy painting), I felt compelled to offer to drive to Hays and help him. And for some other unknown reason, he accepted my offer. I guess maybe I was only half serious and maybe didn't think he would say yes, but he did, so I went. I left the kids with my parents and drove to Hays that next morning to help him paint his living room.

This would now be the third time we had met face to face, and it was much nicer than always texting, Facebook messaging, or even talking on the phone. Plus, we had no distractions from kids or anyone else. Scott was definitely a talker, which was fine because I was a good listener. I also got to witness how he reacted under pressure. When he moved his refrigerator away from the wall to paint behind it, the water line disconnected, and water started spraying everywhere. It was actually quite comical. All in all, if it's possible to have a good time painting, we actually had a fun day, which we both really needed.

We were both enjoying the time so much that I actually didn't even want to leave. I was going to have to leave pretty early in the afternoon in order to get home before dark, since I was still far from comfortable about driving in the dark. I decided to suggest that maybe I could just stay in Hays that night and drive home in the morning. I don't know where it came from, and I felt a little awkward about it, but then again I didn't. Scott said I was welcome to stay in one of the kids' rooms, so I called my mom and made sure she was fine keeping the kids, and I decided to stay. Scott offered to buy me dinner for helping him paint, so we went to Applebee's. Of course, we saw people Scott knew, so we joked about what people would think or say. But then again, we didn't really care. As far as we were concerned we were just two good friends having dinner.

That *is* what we were, right? Just good friends. Well, yes, that's what we were. It was way too soon for either one of us to even consider having romantic feelings toward someone. Besides, even if I thought maybe it felt like something more, I was sure that there was no way Scott was feeling that way. We were both still way too broken and grieving and couldn't imagine ever loving anyone else the way we loved Jason and Cari. We were just two friends traveling a similar path, who enjoyed talking and being around one another.

A week later, November was gone, and December was here. The first Wednesday in December marked the beginning of rifle season for deer. I came from a hunting family, so I took the hunter safety course when I was a kid and loved going hunting with my dad. I had only ever gone pheasant hunting with a shotgun though, so I had never participated in deer season. My dad and both my brothers hunted deer every year, but I never had. In fact, since Jason wasn't a hunter, we rarely ever went back home for a hunting season, so I had not hunted in years.

This year, though, I decided I wanted to shoot a deer. Revenge, maybe? I don't know about that, but the truth of the matter was that the deer population was out of control in our area, so I decided maybe I could save a life if there were fewer deer to jump in the road. I also thought it might be therapeutic and help with my grieving process. So I went hunting with my dad and my brother. It actually ended up being fun and even exciting. I wasn't "trophy hunting" for the "big one" by any means, so I pretty much shot the first deer I saw which was a doe. We donated the meat to a local mission, so I felt good about that as well. While I was in Healy deer hunting with my dad, Scott was back in Beloit deer hunting with his dad and a group of friends who hunt together annually. We enjoyed texting each other back and forth that weekend with deer hunting updates.

Chapter 26

Weekend to Remember

When Jason and I moved away from Hays and I left Hays Med, my good friend and coworker at the time filled my job as clinical instructor. It was a tradition at Hays Med that when the radiology students finished their clinical rotation in December, the clinical instructor would organize a banquet and party for them. Because we had stayed in close touch and also because my friend knew that being around people was really good for me at that point, she invited me to come stay with them and enjoy the party.

At first, I wasn't sure if I wanted to be around all those people and have them all feeling sorry for me and whatnot, but then I thought maybe Scott would be around, and we could get together. When I first told him that I was thinking about coming to Hays the second weekend in December, he had already made plans to go back to Beloit for the weekend again to hunt. Even though I was a little disappointed he would not be in town, I decided that it would still be fun to visit Hays and enjoy an evening with friends. It was always good for me to have things to look forward to, as they made my days and weeks pass by faster. The party was going to be Friday night, so my plan was to drop the kids off at my parents and head to Hays early in the afternoon.

Much to my surprise, Scott called to say that he was thinking about staying in Hays Friday night and heading to Beloit early Saturday morning. He wanted to know if I wanted to have an early dinner before my party. His mom was actually coming to Hays to stay with his kids and take them to a school carnival, since Scott just wasn't up for it, so the kids would be taken care of already. Of course, it sounded like a great idea to me, so Scott suggested that I just come by his house when I got to town, and we could go to dinner from there. I would be able to meet his mom, and it would be fun to see his kids again.

Until now, the date December 12 had no special significance. Little did I know that was about to change, and the date would soon become very significant in this story.

I was really excited and looking forward to my weekend in Hays. I realized during my drive there that I was nervous. But why? It was almost a "butterflies in my stomach" nervous, which was weird. Scott and I had been talking a lot lately. We were texting multiple times a day and then either messaging on Facebook or even visiting on the phone in the evenings. We always had lots to talk about. He was really helpful too, with a lot of issues that we both had to deal with, such as credit card companies, loans, and other bills that were in Jason's name. I was still pretty overwhelmed with a lot of that stuff, so it was nice to have Scott's input and guidance on what I should do, since he had experienced much of it himself. Overall, it was just nice to have someone to visit with. We had both missed that interaction with spouses, and so in a way it was if we still had it. We talked about anything and everything, and it was very comfortable. We even talked about dating—not each other, of course, but just in general.

One evening we were messaging through Facebook, and out of the blue I asked if he had thought about what it would be like to date again. He said he hadn't really thought about it, even though friends had mentioned setting him up. Also a couple of women he knew in Hays had randomly approached him "just to talk," but he sensed that they had an agenda. For some reason, jealousy welled up in me, and I wasn't even sure why. Perhaps I suddenly feared that if he met a woman and started dating again, he wouldn't need or want to talk to me anymore, and I didn't know if I could handle that. He was the only person in the world who understood me, the only person I even wanted to talk to. To lose that would be devastating to me. Then it dawned on me: could it be that I had feelings for him?

My plan for that evening, once I arrived in Hays, was to pick him up at his house so I could see the kids and meet his mom. The kids were adorable and sweet and acted happy to see me, even though they had only met me once before. It really made my day. It was great to meet his mom too. I had no idea exactly what he had told her about me, so I was a bit nervous. We decided that a steak sounded good, so we went to a sports bar that I had never eaten at before called Thirsty's. It was a large and busy place, so we felt very comfortable that we would blend in and not catch a lot of attention. Scott and I were still apprehensive about what people would say if they saw us out together.

We had a great meal and great conversation. I did not want it to end, but the party had started, and I thought I'd better get to it. Not thinking he would say yes, I nonchalantly said he could come with me if he wanted, to which he said sure. At once I almost regretted asking him, thinking that it would look really weird for me to walk into the party with a guy. But then again, I didn't really care, plus we were just friends.

As far as social skills go, I knew that Scott was in advertising sales, and I also knew that he liked to visit with people, so from the moment we walked into that party, he did not know a stranger. He definitely fit right in and could talk to anyone. We honestly did not even spend much time around each other, as we were both constantly visiting with people.

It was great for me to catch up with a lot of them since I had not seen them in a while. I remember one conversation in particular with one of my friends that I had gone shopping with a few weeks earlier. She asked how I was doing, about the kids, and some other small talk, but then she asked, "So what's the status with Scott? He's really cute and so nice!"

I am pretty sure I blushed. And then I realized that prior to right then, I had never actually looked at him "that way." I mean yes, he was a very good-looking guy, but I guess I had never actually considered being physically attracted to him. I told her that we were just friends who obviously had a lot in common right now. But after that conversation, I found myself constantly keeping an eye on him and half-wishing it were just the two of us as I was starting to feel a bit overwhelmed with the crowd. It finally got late enough that everyone started to leave, and once my friend and her husband went to bed, it was just Scott and me. We talked for a little while, and then I suggested that I should probably take him home since he was planning to leave early in the morning.

I hated to see the night end, as we really had a lot of fun together. We sat outside his house in my car visiting for a while longer—just small talk, mostly about hunting, kids, and Christmas coming up. Finally Scott said he had better try and get a little sleep and thanked me for the evening. I thanked him as well, especially for coming to the party with me, and then he leaned over the console to give me a goodbye hug. We hugged and then out of nowhere I gave him a kiss.

What did I just do? I was instantly embarrassed and could not believe my behavior. That was totally unlike me. I don't even know where it came from. Neither one of us said anything other than "bye," and Scott just got out of my car and went inside. I drove off feeling like a complete idiot and very worried about what Scott was thinking. I was beyond mortified. It was way too soon for anything like this, or so I kept trying to tell myself.

I got back to my friend's house and was getting ready for bed when my phone rang. I saw that it was Scott, and I froze. I had absolutely no idea what he wanted, but I was definitely apprehensive to answer. I debated not answering, but then curiosity got the best of me. I answered, and he asked if I was still up. I said yes, and then he asked if he could come back over and talk to me. I said sure and that I would meet him outside.

Talk about an excruciating few minutes waiting for him to get there. I honestly had no idea what he was going to say, but I was really nervous that I had made it awkward and that our friendship would not be the same. He pulled up, and looking back now it was almost like a scene from a movie.

He gets out of his truck and walks up the driveway as I walk toward him. Our eyes meet, and I am speechless, not knowing what it is he is going to say. My instinct is to just apologize, so I start to open my mouth to tell him how sorry I am, and as he approaches me, he says, "I can do better." He then grabs me and gives me the longest, most passionate, knee weakening kiss of my life.

Holy smokes, this was a total game changer. To say I was shocked is an understatement, but I was also pleasantly surprised once the shock wore off. Even though I had recently started to wonder whether I might have "feelings" for him, I was just sure that he did not feel the same way. I was convinced that he considered us good friends helping each other through a very tough time, and that was it. The butterflies were definitely flying now. We ended up staying up most of the night talking about what we were feeling and where we would go from here.

Chapter 27

More than Just Friends

Where would we go from here? It was definitely a lot to process all of a sudden. The next day I had plenty of windshield time to myself on my drive home to try and wrap my head around what this meant. Was it actually possible that this was God's plan? Was it too soon? What would people say or think? A little-known fact about me is that I look for signs ... no not road signs, but signs to help me decide if something is meant to be or not. Well if cheesy love songs were a sign, then it was definitely meant to be, because that was all I heard on the radio on that trip home. One thing I did know for certain: I felt hope again. I felt excitement. I felt happiness and joy, and I felt alive. Surely these were "signs" sent by God.

So often in life we question why? Such a small word, yet probably the biggest question we all face, often daily. Why do I feel this way? Why did you do that? Why do bad things happen? Why, why, why? Not a day goes by that I don't ask myself why—whatever it is—and yet seldom do I actually get an answer. Not an immediate answer anyway. Thinking back, I had questioned "why" a lot over that past year. "Why could I not get pregnant? Why were we in a freak accident? Why did my husband have to die?"

When this "bad stuff" happens to us or around us, it's easy to constantly ask why. We want answers. We want everything to have a reason and make sense. We want to be able to control situations and ultimately our lives. We are humans, and it's our nature to want these things. We just want to be happy, right, but why do things happen to us that prevent us from being happy or joyful, or even content?

We can question all we want, but chances are we may never receive the answers that we so desperately desire. Is it because we are hurting so much that we think an answer or an explanation will take the hurt away? But would it? Does it? It becomes our focus, and when we focus on something, it's often all we can see, and everything else around us becomes too blurry to acknowledge.

I had been there, and no matter how hard I prayed to have peace, those burning "why" questions haunted me. I definitely needed to switch my focus and learn to trust God. It is often in retrospect that we do see the answers to some of those "why" questions or at least see that God had a hand in it all along. It may not have been our plan or what we thought our lives would look like, but sometimes we can definitely see in retrospect that God had a hand in it the entire time.

I once heard that faith is being sure of something we can't see and that if we truly have faith, then with it comes acceptance. Sometimes we have to step out in faith and trust that even though we question or do not see why something is the way it is, still, God has it all under control. We may not ever see or understand on this side of heaven, but one day when we are standing face to face with our Maker, we will know. Or maybe it won't even matter then.

At this point in my story, though, I was starting to think that maybe God did have a plan all along. It still seemed tragic and sad, but having hope and feeling joy and love in my heart after feeling so broken and lost seemed like a definite answered prayer.

So Scott and I were ... dating. Ugh, how strange did that seem for a thirty-year-old mom of a four-year-old and three-month-old? As comfortable as we were with each other, it was still awkward. It's kind of hard to explain, but in a way, we both felt as if we were cheating. I guess because it was not by our choice that our marriages ended, we felt as though we were still married and that we were cheating on our spouse.

Aside from all that, we were both very nervous about how our families and friends would react. It had just been a little over four and a half months since Jason's death and three and a half since Cari's, so in mathematical terms it was pretty soon. But for some reason, especially when we were together, we didn't care. After being so broken and sad it felt so good to have that companionship again. We both questioned ourselves about whether our feelings were genuine or we were just trying to fill a void. But no matter how much we played devil's advocate within our own minds, we wholeheartedly had genuine feelings for one another.

We talked with both sets of our parents right away about our "relationship." We actually had no idea how they would react or what they would say. We braced ourselves for people to talk and for some not to approve. Luckily our parents were not among them. *Relieved* is the word that comes to mind when I think of how they reacted. My mom cried tears of joy, in fact. She then informed me that she did not care what anyone said; if certain people were critical or unsupportive, we should tell them to come talk to her, and she would explain to them how excruciating and heartbreaking it was to watch her daughter go through what I did.

As I have mentioned, my mom has a very strong faith and so she had actually prayed for something like this, and she felt her prayer had been answered. As young as we were, both sets of parents did not want to see us go through life alone or our children to have single parents. Not that marriage was even a thought as of yet, but you know what I mean. It was definitely a relief to have our parents blessing and support. But we still had Jason and Cari's families to tell.

Of course, Jason's family knew of Scott because of his sister Linda's friendship with Cari. And Cari's parents had also learned of Linda's brother's death as well through knowing Linda and seeing her at the family viewing. Scott had also told them that he and I had become friends. Much to our relief, they all gave us their blessing.

Now I don't know honestly deep down how they really felt about it, but regardless, the Kanaks accepted Scott as being a part of my and my kid's lives and the Winebrenners the same for me. There were definitely people along the way that questioned it. I think only because they were very protective brothers, both my brothers as well as Cari's brother had a bit of a hard time with the news. A few friends were apprehensive as well. I don't blame them for their concern as it was out of love, but in our defense, we still held tight to the belief that no one else knew what this journey felt like but us.

There was definitely no rule book written for this type of situation, even though I somedays wish there was a more explicit rule book on life. (Yes, of course there is the Bible, but I couldn't find a place in the Bible that specifically addressed "appropriate and acceptable waiting time for a widow to begin dating again.") I really do believe that "gut feeling" is a "thing." If I pray about something and then I experience a gut feeling, either good or bad, toward something, then I believe that is God speaking to me through the Holy Spirit. Some may argue and others may say they have never felt his way, but I believe it to be true for myself. So, having prayed about Scott and where God intended for him to be in my life, I felt very strongly that this situation was right. And that was all the assurance I needed.

This new level of support that Scott and I had for each other could not have come at a better time. We were both dreading the approaching Christmas holiday. The "firsts" without Jason and Cari had already been hard, and we knew that Christmas would be no different. Jason absolutely loved Christmas. He loved shopping for people as well as spoiling Jaren and me. Plus, we had our annual traditions with both families, and the thought of him not being here this year was devastating. Shopping for the kids, especially for a new baby on her first Christmas, did take my mind off things a bit and put a little excitement in my heart.

Thank God for my kids. As I've said, they were definitely the little blessings that got me through the day and made me keep going. I knew I had to be strong for them and make their needs and happiness my number-one priority. It would be selfish of me not to. I honestly do not know what I would have done without them—or the rest of my family and friends for that matter.

As dark and depressed as I found myself at times, I truly have a greater appreciation for what people that choose to end their life go through. The pain is so unbearable, or you think it is, and you see absolutely no way to make the pain stop other than ending your life. Life itself seems hopeless. I admit, I had never understood how anyone could end their own life, but after going through what I had experienced, I could definitely relate. So I do wonder what might have happened had I not had my faith to begin with, but also my kids, and the support of my family and friends, especially Scott.

We all knew Christmas was going to be extremely difficult. But that didn't take away from the fact that family was always important to us and that we still all wanted to get together. Because I knew how much Jason loved Christmas and getting together with family, I knew he would have wanted it that way. I just kept imagining how much he would have loved buying gifts for Jaren at his age plus spoiling a baby girl on her first Christmas, even though she would be completely oblivious to it.

Our families were all in agreement, though, that maybe we ought to stray from our normal traditions and just go with what we were comfortable with. I did not think I would be comfortable going to Atwood, so Jason's family offered to come to Scott City to celebrate Christmas a few days before the actual holiday. There were definitely tears, but there were also happy tears as we reminisced and shared memories and stories. It was fun to watch Jaren and get the two new babies (mine and Linda's) together for their first Christmas.

I knew that I did not want to spend Christmas Eve alone and wake up Christmas morning alone either, so the kids and I spent Christmas Eve with my family in Healy. Again, it was something we didn't normally do, which made it easier not to dwell on the fact that something (or someone) was missing.

As much as Scott and I would have loved to just skip Christmas and be able to spend time with each other, we knew that we had to be there for our kids and families as well. We did make plans, though, to get together the day after Christmas and spend the weekend together. Having that to look forward to definitely made things a little cheerier.

Scott suggested that it might be fun to go somewhere like Kansas City for the weekend. I had never been to The Plaza during the holidays, so we decided that would be something new and fun for us to do together. His sister and her husband live in Kansas City as well, so he thought it would be fun to get together with them too. I was a little nervous to start meeting more of the family, just because I still was not sure how everyone felt about the situation. My parents were happy to keep my kids for the weekend, and Scott made arrangements for his kids to stay with Cari's parents, which also meant that I would have the opportunity to meet them as well. So it was going to be a pretty big weekend, to put it mildly!

I have to admit I was pretty nervous. A weekend trip together, plus meeting Scott's sister *and* Cari's parents—I felt like this was a pretty big deal and might be a big test to whether this "relationship" was truly in our best interest. Again, as so often in life, the anticipation of something and the "what ifs" can be more stressful than the actual situation turns out to be. We ended up having a wonderful time, except that Scott ended up with strep throat which then resulted in me getting strep throat the next week. That definitely wasn't so wonderful. But Scott's sister and brother-in-law were a lot of fun and very accepting of me, and I could tell instantly that Cari's parents were pretty amazing people. My heart definitely went out to them; I just could not imagine losing your daughter and then being so accepting and welcoming to the "new woman" in their son-in-law's and grandkids' lives. Again, looking back I just feel so very blessed by how our families and friends accepted our relationship and were truly happy for us. I have personally known people and instances in which the family was not so accepting and supportive.

Chapter 28

The Devil on My Shoulder

The next few months definitely had their ups and downs. It felt like a constant struggle to discern between God's plan for my life and the roadblocks that Satan kept throwing out—except that at the time I hardly realized or even considered that it was Satan. Up to this point, I was familiar with Satan biblically, but I never really considered him to be a major factor in my life. Over the years as my faith has grown, and I have personally witnessed God's hand in the events of my life, I have also learned to recognize how Satan works as well.

I think that, in terms of our thoughts and feelings, good is from God and bad is from Satan. Guilt, worry, fear, doubt, anger, sadness—all of which I had felt and we all feel from time to time—can become overwhelming to result in our turning away from God. Why? Maybe because we blame Him for our situation or our feelings. Or maybe we don't feel He was or is there for us. We might feel He isn't answering our prayers or has allowed something bad to happen to us. I admit, in the middle of this trial of my life, I felt that way some days, and it was hard to be trusting and faithful.

But looking back, I am thankful that, no matter what, God was faithful to me. He did not leave me or forsake me, and He did not cause or allow this situation. I believe that God loves us so much that His heart breaks when ours do. He wants us to turn to Him for the comfort and healing that only He can provide. So what gets in the way of that? Satan. He thrives when we question or doubt God. He thrives when we feel all those negative feelings. He thrives when we turn away from God's teachings and try to control everything in our lives.

Satan does not want us to be happy or content. He wants the exact opposite of everything God wants for us. But it is up to us to make that determination. Do we want to follow God, or do we want to let Satan control us? It's definitely not easy but with faith all "things" are possible—these "things" being God's promises.

I found it easy some days to fall into a major funk and allow Satan to control all my thoughts. Even though I had the newfound hope of a new relationship, the fact that it was a long-distance relationship made it difficult. I still felt alone a lot of days. I still missed Jason a lot. I was still sad that he was gone, had never gotten to meet his daughter, and would not get to physically see our kids grow up.

There were many days I felt sorry for myself. I often felt as though everyone around me had been able to just continue on with their daily lives and normal routine and had forgotten all about me and what I was going through. I don't hold that against anyone, because why shouldn't they? But when you are sad and feeling sorry for yourself, it's easy to think like that. I even started to question whether Scott and I should even be in a relationship. Maybe it was too soon. Maybe the feelings really weren't genuine, that they were just to fill a void. How was it ever going to work out anyway? I lived in Scott City, and he lived two hours away in Hays. I had a life here, and he had a life there.

Besides that, some days it just felt awkward. We would be talking and he would talk about Cari or tell a story about her, and an overwhelming sense of never being able to compare to her would come over me. When he talked about her, I felt he placed her up on a pedestal, which I found both sweet and intimidating at the same time. When you have been with someone for seven-plus years as we both had been, you get comfortable. The newness of dating can be far from comfortable, or at least that was what I had convinced myself to think. In all actuality it's the thoughts that run through our head that make it uncomfortable. But nonetheless, I found myself feeling uncomfortable and doubting the relationship. When I am uncomfortable with something I often avoid it, so the distance between us made it easy somedays to avoid it. Scott sensed something was bothering me, even though I tried to act as if everything was fine.

I may have mentioned that Wednesdays were hard for me. The accident happened on a Wednesday, so almost every Wednesday I would replay the whole situation over in my head. Well, this particular Wednesday I felt as though I had fallen into a deep dark pit. My emotions were a mess with thinking about the accident and everything that had happened since then and then trying to rationalize a new relationship despite my doubts. I was just lying on my couch when the doorbell rang. I felt annoyed that someone would be coming by on this Wednesday, of all days, when all I wanted to do was just wallow in my pit by myself.

I opened the door to see Scott standing there. I can't even describe the wave of emotions that suddenly came over me. It was as if all the doubt and self-pity I had been wallowing in had suddenly vanished when I opened the door and saw him standing there. This amazing man, knowing I was having a really rough day and sensing that I was questioning everything going on in my life at that moment, took the day off and drove two hours just to spend literally one hour with me before he had to turn back around and drive back to Hays in time to pick up his kids.

This was monumental for me. I took it as a message to me from the Lord. It was as if God had opened my eyes, and I could finally see Satan behind all that negativity and doubt. He was trying to draw me away from the plan that God had intended for my life.

I sat down with Scott that day and poured my heart and soul out to him, with everything I had been feeling. I admitted that I was intimidated by his relationship with Cari and didn't like wondering if I could ever compare or measure up. He assured me that he understood my concerns, but that he thought that I would think highly of him for placing her up on that pedestal because that meant that I, too, would have my own pedestal. It wasn't as if we would have to share a pedestal. He also shared that he was feeling some of the same doubts and insecurities that I was toward my relationship with Jason. Once again, we were totally on the same page; we just had not communicated it until now. That impromptu visit from Scott was a key turning point in our relationship.

Long-distance relationships are hard and ours was no exception. Seeing each other on the weekends definitely gave us something to look forward to during the week, but then having to leave and go home was difficult. We were both much happier when we were together. I think the biggest frustration for both us of was the single parenting aspect of our situation. It was stressful and simply hard. Top it off with being lonely, plus the mix of emotions stretching from grief to newfound love and missing each other, and we both felt we were on an emotional roller coaster.

Chapter 29

Moving—Again

That spring, Scott's sister and her husband invited us to go on a trip to Florida with them. We both thought that a vacation and the time spent with each other would be really good for us. My doubts about our relationship had subsided, but I felt the trip would be another good test.

We had an amazing time. Spending an entire week together was indescribable. The hardest part about it was coming home and knowing that we would be going our separate directions again and back to a weekend relationship. Following that trip, I knew without a doubt that something had to change. We needed to be together, in the same town, as a couple and as a family. As much as I loved being close to my family, there were just too many memories and reminders of Jason and our life together in Scott City. Since Scott's business was in Hays and was well established, it just made sense for me to be the one to move. This is what I had decided in my own head anyway. I still had to break the news to Scott.

His lack of enthusiasm when I first approached him with these thoughts was discouraging. Scott had told himself that he needed to wait a year after Cari's death before making any major life-changing decisions, and it had not been a year. I guess in a way I felt misled, so then once again I questioned the relationship. I knew in my heart that it was meant to be. I loved him, and he loved me, and we were miserable apart.

I expected him to be excited that I was willing to leave my life in Scott City and move to Hays to be with him. I believe ultimately, he was; he just couldn't shake the expectation of waiting a year that he had placed on himself. And there was still the worry of what people would think or say. I reminded him that there is no rule book for this type of situation. If we truly felt that God was guiding us down this path, then that should be all we needed. Besides, no one had walked this path that we were walking, and unless you have gone down the same road as someone, then you cannot truly understand what they are feeling or going through. We decided to follow our hearts and not worry about what anyone thought except ourselves and God.

I knew that if I was going to move, I wanted to be done by the time school started. Jaren would be starting kindergarten, and I didn't want him starting school in Scott City and then either having to transfer or wait an entire year before we moved. Even though I wasn't crazy about the idea and the moral dilemma it involved, I was even willing to move without being engaged or married. We had discussed having two houses, but we knew that eventually we wanted to get married, and it just made sense for us to establish a household from the get-go. Scott's house was way too small to accommodate six of us. Once we started talking seriously about it, while we kept on seeing each other only on the weekends, it did not take much discussion before Scott was on board with me moving.

Luckily it didn't take us too long to find a house that would be a perfect fit for our blended family. So the kids and I packed up our house and moved to Hays in July of 2009. It was bittersweet, to say the least, but we truly felt that it was God's plan for our lives.

Scott and I were really amazed by the many similarities of our previous lives. We all attended college and lived in Hays during the same period. We were both first married in 2001, and both our wedding colors were blue and yellow. This next one always really amazes people when I tell the story. I will never forget the day that we had started packing up Scott's house to move to our new house, and I came across their wedding china. Curious, I opened the box, and believe it or not it was the exact same pattern as mine, only mine had a gold ring around the edge and theirs had a platinum ring. The upshot is that we now have twenty-four place settings of coordinating china.

It was definitely a major adjustment, but we were all so happy to finally be together that we made the best of it. It felt great not to feel so lonely anymore. For the most part, the kids all meshed together well. Benton and Jaren were similar in that they would get easily wound up with other kids around. Jaren had been on his own for four years, so having these other kids in the house was exciting for him.

They all loved having each other to play with. Lilian absolutely loved having a baby sister. She was always wanting to help feed her and dress her and considered her a real-life baby doll. At times they got on each other's nerves, which was understandable considering how drastically their lives had all changed, but it was really nothing out of the ordinary for siblings. At times it was awkward to be called Lisa and for Jaren and Lynsi not to be technically able to refer to Scott as Dad. But nevertheless we made it work. Part of my heart was still broken for these children, and I often worried about Benton and Lilian accepting me as "Mom" someday. Scott must have felt the same about Jaren. Lynsi was not going to know any differently.

We decided that under the circumstances it would be best for me to be a stay-at-home mom. I preferred the term Domestic Goddess, but soon realized the gig was far from goddess status. But again, I felt strongly that it was my purpose for this season of life we were in.

I really did enjoy the opportunity to be at home with the two girls, since I had always worked full-time. Having girls was definitely a new experience for me. Lilian was all about being a princess; she loved the color pink and anything that sparkled! I didn't have any sisters growing up, and I was a bit of a tom boy and up to this point, I had only had a son so you can imagine my lack of experience. I was used to cars, superheroes, and roughhousing, and now my repertoire was being expanded to include baby dolls, Barbies, Disney princesses, and playing dress-up, every day, *all* day. It was amazing. If only to be a kid and live in a pretend world half the time.

While the girls and I spent a good portion of our day in what came to be known as "Lili-land," the boys were both adjusting well to kindergarten and third grade. We worried a lot about them, since they were the two oldest and understood the most. You really never know how a trauma like this will affect a child. As it happened, they both adjusted very well. In fact, they both had hobbies that I think, looking back, really took their minds off things and helped with their healing. Benton loved to read and could already read at a sixth-grade level. His little mind was like a sponge. He could read something or just hear it and remember it. He amazed me. If you didn't know where Benton was, he could always be found somewhere reading or watching the Discovery channel (or both simultaneously).

Jaren's favorite things about kindergarten seemed to be recess and PE. That boy has always been active and energetic. I had a feeling he was going to be athletic as well. However, he had also developed a love for drawing. Not coloring or painting or any other aspect of art so much, just mostly drawing. His drawings were actually very good for a five-year-old. He was always drawing pictures for people, and he could draw anything! In kindergarten they do a career program where they dress up and portray what they want to be when they grow up. Jaren dressed up as an artist, which was a welcome surprise; I'd been sure he would choose Superman or Spiderman.

Chapter 30

Joining Our Lives Officially

Scott and I had talked about marriage, and we both knew that it was something we wanted. I didn't want to push the issue, and I really wasn't in a hurry. I knew our moving in together was a huge step in and of itself. So you can imagine my surprise when Scott planned a weekend getaway to Kansas City the first part of September and ended up proposing to me.

I noticed that he was acting odd, but I didn't think much of it. He had booked us a room at The Sheraton on The Plaza, the same hotel we had stayed in when we took our first weekend trip together back in December. When we arrived to check in, we learned they had overbooked and did not have a room for us. However, they did make a complimentary reservation for us at another hotel on The Plaza. Scott seemed disappointed and a bit annoyed, which seemed peculiar to me considering we were getting a free night's stay.

We headed over to the Intercontinental Hotel to check in. This hotel even had a bellman who took our bags for us and would bring them to our room. We checked in and went up to check out our room.

This hotel was very nice, and we had an amazing view of The Plaza from our room.

At this point Scott was about to wear a path in the floor from pacing the room. I asked him what was wrong with him, and he just said it was making him nervous that our bags were not there yet. Again, I thought he was being weird but didn't think much of it. Finally the luggage arrived, and he seemed relieved and soon calmed down.

Once we were settled, we decided to walk to The Plaza and have dinner. Scott suggested the Cheesecake Factory because he knew it was my favorite. At this point, I did wonder if he had something planned, but there was no proposal during dinner. I might have been slightly disappointed, but again I honestly had no idea if he was even ready yet, so I didn't let on that I was disappointed.

After a wonderful dinner and nice walk through The Plaza, we went back to the hotel. We were lying on the bed watching a movie when Scott got up and went to the bathroom. When he came back, I noticed that he walked over to his suitcase, but then I didn't pay much attention to what he was doing. The next thing I knew, I spotted him out of the corner of my eye, and he was on the floor. I quickly sat up and asked if he had fallen—and then I realized what he was doing. He was on one knee holding the ring in front of me.

He said, "Tonight didn't go anywhere near how I had planned, but despite all that, you and I being together is what I want forever. Will you marry me?" He then proceeded to tell me about his original plan and how having to switch hotels had thrown a kink into it. He had booked the exact same room at The Sheraton where we had stayed previously, so he was very disappointed when that didn't work out. Then the reason he was so nervous about our bags not showing up to the new room was because the ring was in his suitcase. His behavior all day made total sense now.

Oh, and I said yes.

We were married a month later, on October 24. Yep, I planned a wedding in a month. We got married in our backyard on a beautiful fall day, and it was perfect. We had both had "the big wedding" the first time, so all we wanted was a small ceremony with family and a reception with family and friends. At this point in our life we realized our union was less about the ceremony and more about the marriage, so there was no need for a big wedding.

We wanted our children to be a part of the ceremony. Benton was a ring bearer and Lilian a flower girl, and they both accompanied Scott down the aisle hand in hand. Jaren was also a ring bearer and Lynsi a flower girl, and the intent was that they would both walk me down the aisle. However, Lynsi—being only one and barely walking—decided she would rather sit in the middle of the aisle and play with the flower petals. So my best friend and personal attendant, Gina, carried Lynsi the rest of the way while Jaren held my hand and walked me down the aisle. We asked Jason's sister, Linda, to be our matron of honor and Cari's brother Erick to be best man, and Pastor Dennis from Scott City performed the ceremony.

It was truly a wonderful day. Our families—all four sides—were all very happy for us and cried tears of joy. It was even clearer that everything up to this point had been perfectly orchestrated by God. He had taken this broken situation and turned it into something beautiful. Although sad and tragic at first, it seems that things do happen for a reason and that some things are truly meant to be.

I think my favorite part was our wedding vows. They were definitely not traditional, but they were perfect for us and our situation.

> Lisa, because of you, I laugh, I smile, I dare to dream again. I look forward with great joy to spending the rest of my life with you, caring for you, nurturing

you, being there for you in all life has in store for us, and I vow to be true and faithful for as long as we both shall live.

I promise to be a good and faithful husband to you, and also a patient, loving father to Jaren and Lynsi, caring for them and providing for them as my own. I promise to be their strength and their emotional support, loving them with all my heart forever.

Scott, because of you, I laugh, I smile, I dare to dream again. I look forward with great joy to spending the rest of my life with you, caring for you, nurturing you, being there for you in all life has in store for us, and I vow to be true and faithful for as long as we both shall live.

I promise to be a good and faithful wife to you, and also a patient, loving mother to Benton and Lilian, caring for them and providing for them as my own. I promise to be their strength and their emotional support, loving them with all my heart forever.

It was a beautiful ceremony followed by a wonderful reception with even more family and friends. The last time so many of our family members and friends had gathered was to "celebrate" the lives of two people, but for a much different reason. Yes, many of us hadn't seen one another since the funerals the previous year. The joining of our two lives that day felt much more like a celebration should, and we felt abundantly blessed by the love and support we were shown, not just that day but over the past year as well.

I would like to be able to tell you that we lived happily ever after and were never faced with a trying or challenging test of faith again. But these tests are what contribute to our testimony. It's not always easy to trust and be faithful while we are going through the storm. Still, often as we look back and see what our trials have taught us about ourselves, our faith, and God's never-ending love and faithfulness to us, we receive hope and the strength to persevere.

It can be mind-boggling how much life can change in the blink of an eye. When you break it down, that entire year of my life was a roller coaster of emotions—from being pregnant and involved in a traumatic accident that claimed the life of my husband and made me a widowed single mom battling severe depression, to finding love again, dating, moving, getting married, and going from a mom of one to a mom of four. It was all pretty unbelievable when you think about it. I was ready to just feel "normal" again and focus on being the best wife and mother I could be, seeing as how I'd been given what I felt was a second chance.

I soon realized that "normal" is just a setting on the washing machine. My expectations of being the perfect stay-at-home housewife and mom far outweighed my abilities. I tried to have a positive attitude and be thankful, but it wasn't as if this new life guaranteed smooth sailing and abundant happiness and joy. It was hard work.

Being a blended family was a challenge in itself. As a mother, I struggled with trying to be fair and love everyone equally, even though I did not give birth to two of these children and had only really known them less than a year. I soon learned that love is not one size fits all, and there are many different forms of love. As a child, I dreamed of one day being a wife and a mother, and I wanted four kids. Obviously, that was before I had ever had kids at all. Chances are, had life not gone down this path, I might have stopped at two. Who knows? Only God. Obviously, this was the plan He intended for me as a mother.

It wasn't long before I started referring to the children as "the Fab Four." It was as if we had our own little gang of superheroes, because in my eyes, they truly were little superheroes, and Scott and I were

Super Dad and Super Mom. We truly had a whole new identity and purpose in life. Even though we still had difficult days and still dealt with grief, we had a responsibility to raise these children.

As time went on, I began to feel more adjusted to our new life. However, I felt something was missing. I soon realized it was church. I had always been very involved in church, specifically the Methodist church, as I grew up attending it. I always felt uplifted and closer to God when I was in church and involved in church activities. Scott had grown up in the Presbyterian church, but he and Cari had not attended church in Hays regularly. I had actually been a member of the First United Methodist church in Hays, and in fact, that was where Jason and I were married.

Not wanting to push the issue on Scott, as he was still struggling with his faith at this point, I expressed my desire to attend church as a family. I was willing to compromise on what church we attended as long as we just started going. Scott's kids had been attending the Wednesday kids' program and Lilian's preschool was at the First Presbyterian Church, so he suggested we attend services there. We tried it a few times, but I just did not feel at home. Maybe I was being closed-minded, but I just had this "once a Methodist, always a Methodist" frame of mind. I finally got the nerve to communicate my feelings to Scott; although he was apprehensive, knowing it was important to me, he agreed to try the Methodist church.

Despite his feelings at the time, he knew we both wanted our children to be involved in and "grow up" in the church. I instantly felt back home. From the pastors to the people, to just being in that building, I had an immediate sense of comfort and peace. I truly felt God had led me (us) back to this church at just the right time.

As I mentioned, life was maybe not everything I expected it to be, and I started to struggle emotionally. I hadn't talked to anyone or done any counseling since meeting with Pastor Dennis in Scott City.

I decided to reach out to the associate pastor at the church, who also happened to be a woman as well as a wife and a mom. After just a few sessions with her, it was clear to me that God did indeed have a plan for me to be back at this church and be mentored by this amazing woman. It's as if she always knew exactly what to say to either make me feel better or help me see things from a new perspective.

I honestly felt she was a vessel through which God was directly speaking to me. God truly places people in our lives for a reason. To this day I still carry with me much of what she taught. She was the first person to really help me see how Satan tries to control our feelings and emotions. In one particular meeting, all I kept talking about were my feelings of guilt in many areas of my life. She introduced me to the concept that guilt and many other negative feelings are from Satan. They are not from God. I was very blessed by this woman and how she helped me view my life with a whole new perspective.

She was also the reason I joined the women's Bible study group. She was leading a group and encouraged me to join and get involved with other women in our church. I had no idea how much of an impact being involved in that women's Bible study would have on my faith walk and spiritual growth. I formed amazing friendships with the ladies and always left study feeling uplifted and encouraged. After attending a couple different study sessions, a dear friend and I were asked if we would be interested in taking over the group as coleaders. What an amazing opportunity that turned out to be, not only leading the group but coleading with one of my best friends.

Although very bittersweet, both my pastor and my friend eventually moved away from Hays. It was bitter because I hated to see them go, as they both were special to me and had such a huge impact on my life, but sweet because they had both been presented with wonderful new career opportunities. But thanks to them both, the groundwork for my role as women's Bible study leader was laid, and as I write this almost eight years later, I still have the pleasure and honor of being the leader of "GAB" (girlfriends and the Bible) at our church.

And speaking of career opportunities, it didn't take me long to realize how much I truly missed working outside the home. I loved working in radiology as well as the interaction with patients and coworkers. I had determined that the modality of radiology I would be most interested in working in again was mammography. In June 2010, an "as needed" part-time position became available, and I jumped at the opportunity. It was perfect for me. I could still be primarily a stay-at-home mom but could also get back out in the working world and have adult interaction doing what I was educated to do.

Chapter 31

He Carried Me

A couple years later, in 2011, I had been having some abdominal pain that I thought might be my gallbladder. I went to the doctor, and she ordered a sonogram to check my gallbladder. My gallbladder was fine, but the sonogram showed an area on my liver that needed a CT scan to better visualize. The area on my liver was normal but the scan, showed a spot on my right kidney that looked a little suspicious. It was very small, but they were uncertain what it was. I then needed an MRI to better evaluate my kidney.

From the radiologist's recommendation, my doctor determined that we could just monitor it every six months and do another scan to check it. After a year and a half, it had slowly but gradually grown in size. The radiologist was concerned and suggested I see a specialist. The specialist here in Hays thought that it would probably be best to have the area on my kidney removed, but it was not something he would be able to do. We then traveled to KU Med in Kansas City to see another specialist. He agreed that I should have it removed. He said that there was no way to know whether it was cancer without removing it and testing it. They were hopeful that they could just remove that small part of my kidney, but there was no guarantee; it was a possibility that once they got in there, they would have to take my entire kidney.

Surgery was scheduled for April 18, 2013. I was scared to death. I knew in my head that God would be with me and the doctors, but my heart and my emotions were a mess. Other than my wisdom teeth, I had never had surgery, so the thought of a major operation terrified me. But the thought of it being cancer scared me more, so I accepted that it needed to be done. I was scheduled to have a pre-op appointment in Kansas City again a few weeks before the surgery. We decided that we would just make a fun family weekend out of it and take the kids to Great Wolf Lodge (indoor water park). Maybe that would relieve some stress as well. Stress and I do not get along. I often get physically ill from too much stress, so incidentally I had not been feeling well leading up to this appointment.

I also happened to be "late" on my monthly cycle, which I had also attributed to stress. But I thought I had better take a pregnancy test just in case. I knew there was no way I was pregnant because I just didn't get pregnant that easy. I almost passed out from shock when I saw the two lines on that pregnancy test. This was *so not* the plan. I was overwhelmed with four kids the way it was, plus we were happy with things the way they were. We had actually decided not to have any kids together. In fact, Scott had been scheduled for surgery back in February to prevent that but ended up rescheduling it because he wanted to participate in a benefit 5K run honoring Carl. And I was supposed to have surgery in a few weeks to remove what could be a cancer from my kidney. I found myself asking how this could be the plan now. But as we have learned, our plan and God's plan are often not the same. This is another one of those examples of how, in retrospect, God's plan and timing were perfect.

Obviously, I did not have the surgery. The doctors did recommend that I have a sonogram of my kidney in mid-pregnancy to check things. That actually opened up a whole new can of worms. The spot had increased in size again, and the radiologists were very concerned at the possibility that if it was cancer, I would need to look into having it removed during the pregnancy. They said considering its location, if it was cancer and continued to grow, it could spread, and then my prognosis would not be good.

I thought I'd been scared before, but after sitting with the radiologist and hearing this information, I was even more terrified. All I could do was pray. I begged God for peace and comfort. I prayed that it wasn't cancer. I feared that if it was, I would not survive, and I could not even stomach the thought of Scott and the kids going through loss all over again.

Why was this happening? Why couldn't I just have a "normal", easy pregnancy? I felt so much frustration and disappointment that I could not enjoy this pregnancy, especially since my pregnancy with Lynsi had been stressful as well. We had found out that we were having another little girl which I suspected by the similarities to how I'd felt with Lynsi. What should have been an exciting time of shopping, decorating a nursery, and looking forward to experiencing the birth of my daughter with Scott was instead nine long months of doctor's appointments, stress, worry, fear, and exhaustion.

My doctor at Hays arranged for me to see another specialist in Denver. This specialist happened to be a woman, which actually gave me some sense of comfort. At this point, being pregnant and excessively emotional meant that I felt as though all the male doctors I was seeing were insensitive to my situation. Knowing I would be seeing a female doctor was very encouraging to me. The fact that she was a "urologic oncologist" was not so comforting—I knew that oncologists treat cancer—but nonetheless I was trying to stay positive. I just continued to pray for comfort.

I sometimes do this weird thing when I pray. I ask God for a sign. I found myself praying for signs during this time. Even on the long car ride to Denver, I was constantly praying and asking for peace. I often look to the sky and the clouds. I love to look for shapes within the clouds. As we were driving into the outskirts of Denver, a huge cloud formed in the unmistakable shape of a heart. The next sign came when we walked into the doctor's office. The receptionist's computer had a big orange sticker on the back of it with a Denver Broncos mascot and the words "united in orange." I instantly felt as if it was a message from my guardian angel.

The last sign of the day might be the strangest story you have ever heard and might just convince you that I must be crazy. But I am going to tell the story anyway. As we are sitting in the exam room waiting for the doctor, a small spider crawled across the room right in front of me. I normally would not hesitate to step on a spider when I see one inside because I worry about spider bites. However, for some reason all I could do was sit and watch this spider. It stopped right in front of me and just sat there.

You might be thinking, *Big deal; there was a spider in the room.* But this was not an ordinary spider. I had never seen a spider like this before. This spider was seriously a deep orange-red color. Again with the orange ... it had to be a message of comfort from Jason. But the craziest part of this story is that when the doctor finally walked in the room, her hair color was the exact same color as that spider. Yep—crazy, right?

Anyway, this doctor was *amazing.* Much to our relief, she encouraged us that, first of all, she did not think it was cancer, and second, we did not need to worry about doing anything at this point. She told us to try to enjoy the rest of the pregnancy; once the baby was born, we would reevaluate everything. Scott and I left her office and stood in the hallway hugging and crying. We were so relieved. Our prayers had been answered.

Even with the encouraging news from the doctor in Denver, I would not call the last few months of my pregnancy enjoyable. I feel bad admitting it, but I was not a very good pregnant person. I felt sick all the time. I was beyond exhausted from trying to maintain a household with four other kids. Plus, I just could not shake the stress and worry over the unknowns of this kidney situation. I often allowed Satan to control my thoughts and actions during this time. This was another one of those instances where I had a hard time practicing my faith and being diligent in prayer and devotion.

But looking back on it now, it was also one of those times where I had an abundance of prayer warriors covering me in prayer. "God is always faithful, even when we are faithless" is something that really resonated with me from a Bible study called *When God Doesn't Fix It* by Laura Story. It has been true in my faith journey. From Jason's death to my health and this pregnancy and everything in between, there were definitely times where I know I was not a faithful servant, but no matter what, God was always right there.

The Lord has definitely carried me when I couldn't find the strength to move forward on my own. He has carried me and has always placed just the right people in my life to help me as well. Of course, now my sense of humor has me picturing Jesus carrying this huge pregnant woman. I don't know why my mind does that. If I don't laugh, I may cry, right?

As I neared the final month of my pregnancy I was faced with yet another challenge. Painful and emotional memories and reminders of my pregnancy with Lynsi resurfaced. Some days I was overcome with many different feelings and emotions: fear, sadness, anger, anxiety, and worry, to name a few. Much of my anger stemmed from the fact that prior to facing the tragedy of losing Jason, I never really had a lot of fears. Now, I found myself fearful of having to go through a loss like that again.

Yes, my head knew that my faithful God was with me every step of the way. He had brought me through that trial and would be with me through anything else I might encounter. But my heart was another subject. The head knows what the heart sometimes can't feel, and that was certainly true for me. I knew that worrying about things doesn't keep them from happening, but I couldn't convince my heart not to feel all those feelings. Luckily, though, I had learned that being intentional about prayer and doing devotions helped to calm my anxious heart and subside my worrying. I am pretty sure that I experienced a form of post-traumatic stress syndrome after Jason's death and my pregnancy with Lynsi, and recalling those memories sure made for a difficult last month of this pregnancy.

And to top it all off, in order to add another bedroom to accommodate this new addition, we had completely gutted and were in the process of remodeling our basement. This resulted in our family being confined upstairs, with the boys sharing a room and the two girls sharing the other room. So between construction, construction workers, and us all living on one floor of our home, this pregnant mama was probably not the most pleasant person to be around.

Chapter 32

Bundle of Joy

My original due date was November 17, but after my first sonogram it was moved to November 25. Even though the due date is just a number, I was glad they moved it, as November 17 was my first wedding anniversary, and I just felt like it would be an awkward connection. At first, I was hoping she would come November 10, since both Jaren and Lynsi were born on the 10. Then the more I got to thinking about it, I remembered that Scott and I first met in person back in 2008 on November 16 when he and the kids came to Scott City for the first time. I thought it would be yet another "Godincidence" for her to be born five years to the day after Scott and I met. But I'd been a week overdue with my other two, so I wasn't getting my hopes up.

Much to my surprise, on November 15 I started having "signs" of impending labor. With my other two, once that happened, I gave birth the next day. Then that afternoon I started having contractions. Ironically that same day the workers were putting the final touches on the basement, so we were free to start moving furniture back in. One of the guys that had been doing the remodel graciously offered to help Scott move furniture back in. I had them move the couches in first, and then I sat on the couch, reclined back, and directed where everything needed to go all while having minor contractions.

I continued to have contractions all night, but they were irregular and didn't really increase in intensity or get more frequent, so I knew I didn't need to go to the hospital just yet. The next morning, though, I felt like they were stronger and coming more often, so we went ahead to the hospital. They admitted me, hooked me up to the monitor, and checked my progress. I was surprised to find out that I was only dilated between three and four centimeters. My contractions had somewhat subsided as well. The doctor decided to have me stay so they could monitor me and see if my labor would progress. He said he would check back after lunch unless something progressed sooner. Not much had changed by the time he came back, and I could tell he wasn't quite sure what to tell me.

He then asked me if I wanted to have this baby today or if I wanted to go home. Of course, I wanted to have the baby that day! It was November 16, and it would make for a great addition to our story. So I told him that I would prefer to go ahead and have her, so he broke my water and started me on Pitocin to induce labor. I had been on the fence about whether I wanted an epidural or not. I'd had it with my other two, so I didn't know any different, but I was curious about having a natural delivery.

Little did I know, I was in for the most intense pain I would ever experience. My epidurals with the other two were both fairly early on in labor, so I really did not have any pain or super-intense contractions. I had no idea what it was really like without the drugs masking the pain. I guess maybe part of me thought that there was no physical pain that could be worse than the emotional pain I had experienced. *I. Was. Wrong.*

Each time the nurse came in to check on me, she offered to call Anesthesia if I wanted an epidural, but I kept refusing. I am not really sure what I was trying to prove. As dilation neared eight centimeters, I felt myself becoming one of those screaming, writhing women I used to see on *A Baby Story*, which I'd sworn I would never be.

At that point I finally asked for an epidural. Of course, I think that they just told me they were calling Anesthesia when they knew full well that (1) I was already too far along, and (2) the baby was going to be born before Anesthesia would have time to get there. I could tell I was progressing very quickly at this point, and I needed to get this baby out before I exploded. I had absolutely no control over my body, and I kept telling everyone that this baby was going to come out whether they were ready or not, to which the nurse kept saying, "Just hold on, just wait."

Really? As sweet and nice as she was, she was really lucky that I was able to muster the composure not to kick her because my leg would have been long enough to reach her. I can't even imagine what Scott was thinking at this point. Maybe "what have I gotten myself into" Haha. With the absence of an epidural and being able to FEEL EVERYTHING that was happening was probably both a blessing and a curse. The labor itself was excruciating at times, but the delivery was a piece of cake. The doctor literally walked in and was able to gown and glove up just in time to catch her. At 3:54 p.m. Layci Joy McGrath entered our world and for a moment all the pain I had felt was gone, and I was filled with the most euphoric sense of love. Or maybe it was just relief that the pain was gone, but euphoric love sounds so much sweeter. She was absolutely beautiful and perfect in every way. (said every mother ever). She was truly a gift from God. I immediately felt a new, even stronger bond between Scott and I now that we shared a biological child. Aside from that, she bonded our family in a way that we never imagined, and I now know that God knew that was exactly what we needed. I honestly don't know why I doubted God's plan and timing. I guess I am just human, and His plan is far above our human comprehension.

To say the other kids loved her is a total understatement. I have never seen sibling love like this before. Yes, my kids all loved each other, and they were pretty enamored with Lynsi when she was a baby, but this was just different. Almost unexplainable. It amazed me as a mother to watch each of my children hold this new baby and just smile from ear to ear. They all loved her beyond belief. My heart was full and my cup truly overflowed.

Now what had once been the "Fab Four" would now be lovingly referred to as the "Fab Five." I could not help but think about the phrase *raising arrows*, which I had recently read somewhere. It reminded me of Psalm 127:3–5, which says, "Children are a heritage from the Lord, offspring a reward from him. Like arrows in the hands of a warrior are children born in one's youth. Blessed is the man whose quiver is full of them." I would say our "quiver" was definitely full, and we were abundantly blessed.

A few weeks after Layci's birth, once things had settled down a bit and we had begun to get used to being a family of seven, it was time for me to do something I had been dreading. It was time for me to have my kidney checked. Postpartum emotions were always crazy for me anyway, but they were at an extraordinary level of crazy at this point. On one hand, I was relieved that my pregnancy was over, that delivery had gone well, and that Layci was perfectly healthy. But the fear of the unknown was overwhelming. My thoughts were flooded with endless "what ifs": *What if it has grown? What if I need surgery right away and I have a newborn baby and four other kids to take care of? What if it is cancer? What if I die? What will happen to my family?*

Why is it that in situations like these we often only think of the negative "what ifs"? Is it because we want to try and prepare ourselves for the worst? I think that is what I do. I seem to believe that if I think of all the possible negative scenarios, then they won't actually happen. I never once allowed myself to consider one single positive "what if." I prayed constantly that it had not grown and that it would not be cancer. I had an army of wonderful prayer warriors praying for me as well, but I still never once considered, *What if it shrunk? What if it is gone? What if it is not cancer?* Part of me did not even want to have the scan because maybe it would just be easier if I didn't know. I decided that was crazy, as was most of my thinking during this time. As you can imagine, I didn't have very many rational thoughts at all.

Nevertheless, I put on my big-girl pants and went in for that scan. As I drove to the hospital, I just prayed, asking God to calm my anxious heart and give me peace. I lay down on that ultrasound table and looked away from the screen. I usually liked to watch what they were doing, and they usually allowed it since I was a coworker, and they all knew me. But not today. Today I didn't want to see. I just wanted to have faith and believe in something without seeing it.

The tech started scanning me, and as she was moving the transducer along my side, she let out a faint "huh." Of course, I had to look then, and without even thinking about it I said, "What? What's wrong?"

She then said, "I am having a hard time even finding the spot today." She had me roll into a different position and tried other angles, and finally she was able to find it. She then said, "It's sure not a very big spot; I think it's measuring smaller than last time."

It was all I could do to hold back the tears from the flood of emotion that came over me at that moment. I held my composure until I reached my car, and then the waterworks exploded. I sent Scott a message telling him the good news, and then I called my mom. When she answered, I was bawling and scared her to death, but once I was finally able to put together the words "The spot shrank," she was then crying on the other end of the phone. We sat there and cried over the phone together for I don't know how long.

Once I received word of the official report, I sent my results to the doctor in Colorado. She confirmed that had this been a cancer, it would not have shrunk. She advised I continue to monitor it, but that cancer and surgery were no longer concerns. All I could think about was Layci and how this little bundle of *joy* saved my kidney. Had I not gotten pregnant with her, I would have had an unnecessary surgery and most likely lost my entire kidney. How could this not have all been perfectly orchestrated by such a loving God? My only regret was that I wasted so much time and energy worrying and being fearful of the unknown when I should have trusted God's plan all along. But once again, I am human, and as humans, we find it sometimes difficult to fully trust the unknown. By God's amazing grace I am definitely working on it though.

Chapter 33

Inspired to Persevere

As of May 2018, this book has been a seven-year work in progress. It started out as a personal journal, but along the way I felt that God was encouraging me to share my story with others. Many people know the CliffsNotes version of our story. This version obviously looks more in depth at my faith journey and personal testimony, up to and including the birth of Layci. I would have continued on, but the book might never end, and I had to end it somewhere. Who knows, maybe there will be subsequent books.

As I finish documenting these steps in my journey thus far, the kids are now Benton, 17; Jaren, 14; Lilian, 13; Lynsi, 10; and Layci, 4, and life is absolutely crazy busy. I wish I could tell you we have the perfect storybook life, but I don't think such a life exists. We have good days and bad days, ups and downs, just like everyone. Being a blended family is still challenging for us, but we make it a point to be grateful for the second chance and opportunity we were given.

I admit, we sometimes wonder what might have been, but at the end of the day there is no point in doing that, as nothing can change the plan that God put in place Despite all the tragedy and trying situations we have been through, we truly do consider ourselves beyond blessed to have found one another and blended our families and to be looking forward to our continuing life together. A favorite quote of mine I feel perfectly sums up our life: "Our family is a circle of strength; founded on faith, joined in love, kept by God, together forever." I just love everything about what this says.

My story is a perfect example of how our tests and trials contribute to our testimony. I am amazed daily by how the Lord works in my life and those around me. I have grown a great deal in my faith through all of this and learned lots about life in general. I have developed a deep love for scripture, and find myself completely intrigued by the Bible. It is truly an instruction manual for our lives. I am constantly finding new scriptures that are instantly my "favorite." I have countless "favorites," most of which provided great comfort and encouragement to me in my darkest times and still do.

Second Corinthians 5:7 is my motto. It is tattooed on my foot and displayed on the wall in practically every room of our home. It says, "Walk by faith and not by sight." I think my story here is a prime example of realizing that you can seldom see the path laid out before you, but you keep walking on in faith, knowing that God has already designed it for you.

There is an entire Bible full of amazing and encouraging scriptures, and when I am down or discouraged, I always recommend reading from the book of Psalms for encouragement. However, I am often drawn to find scriptures in books of the Bible that we don't routinely hear. One of my other favorites comes from the book of Nahum, a somewhat dark book, but I do love this verse (1:7): "The Lord is good, a refuge in times of trouble. He cares for those who trust in him." He cares for those who trust in Him. It can be hard to trust especially when you are smack-dab in the middle of a difficult situation. But again, remember, think about all the past situations He has brought you through, and be encouraged by that. So far, my track record for getting past difficult situations is 100 percent, and I give all the glory to God.

How many of you turn to music for inspiration and encouragement? Well, I love music and music speaks straight to my heart. I can almost always think of a song that applies to any situation I am going through and be encouraged by it. If I were to pick a "theme song" for this journey, I would choose "Blessings" by Laura Story. Many friends sent me the link to this song because when they heard it, they thought of me and my story. It is truly an amazing, inspiring song.

A few years ago, I discovered the amazing contemporary Christian artist, Mandisa. She sings a song titled "Overcomer" which is inspired by the following three Scripture verses:

> You, dear children, are from God and have overcome them, because the one who is in you is greater than the one who is in the world. (1 John 4:4)

> For everyone born of God overcomes the world. This is the victory that has overcome the world, even our faith. Who is it that overcomes the world? Only the one who believes that Jesus is the Son of God. (1 John 5:4–5)

> I have told you these things, so that in me you may have peace. In this world you will have trouble. But take heart! I have overcome the world. (John 16:33)

Friends, these all point out that we will have troubles in this life, and Satan will try and test us, but we are overcomers because Jesus was an overcomer. We *are* overcomers, not we *can be* overcomers; we *are* overcomers, and we can overcome any situation because Jesus is on our side.

Before such a life-changing tragic event, I might not have been so impacted by a show like *American Idol* as I was during season 8, which aired that January (2009) after Jason died. There was a contestant on the show by the name of Danny Gokey. Just four weeks before he auditioned for *American Idol*, his wife, Sophia, died from complications during a heart surgery. It was Sophia who loved the show and had encouraged him to audition. How easy it would have been for him to give up on his dream of being a musician after losing the love of his life and biggest encourager!

But he persevered. He went on the show, in her honor, and even though he finished third, he was still offered a record deal. Watching him and listening to his music gave me much hope and encouragement, as did his book, *Hope in Front of Me: Find Purpose in Your Darkest Moments*. I was thrilled to be able to attend one of Danny's concerts, meet him, and obtain an autographed copy of his book.

Another musician who encouraged me because of his testimony following the loss of a spouse was Jeremy Camp. His experience led him to write a song called "Walk by Faith," which you might remember is my life verse. Jeremy also wrote a book, called *I Still Believe*, and shared his life story and spiritual journey. Both these books had a huge impact on me and my outlook following a devastating loss. Their music continues to be a huge inspiration even now. I have seen Jeremy Camp perform three times and Danny Gokey twice, and they do not fail to inspire and encourage me.

In the midst of my trials, past and present, I have found that I am not always good at talking about the bad stuff that clouds my soul. When this happens, I find myself in a dark place. I often feel alone, as if I am the only one who can understand *me*. Plus, I don't want to burden others with my burdens. It's as though I know in my head how I *should be* feeling or acting and how thankful I should be, but my heart won't follow. Luckily, God is bigger than me and my darkness. I find myself praying for Him to send me a message, some encouragement, hope, and yes, the power to turn my light back on.

He never fails me. Ever. As is often the case, it is through music that I feel redeemed. As I am reflecting on what is actually troubling me and once again feeling that no one could possibly know what "all this" feels like, I remind myself: *He knows.* Jeremy sings a song with this exact title, and it is so powerful, it brings tears to my eyes. When we think that no one could possibly know what our burdens and suffering feel like, we need to remember what Jesus's burdens and suffering were like and be reminded that *"He knows."* I am then reminded that no burden that I will ever face can even come close to comparing to what Jesus went through. And He did it all out of love for us.

This scripture contains two of my favorite words, *joy* and *perseverance.* It says, "Consider it pure joy my brothers and sisters, whenever you are faced with trials of many kinds, because you know that the testing of your faith develops perseverance" (James 1:2–3). The book of James teaches us that if we really possess genuine faith, it will not snap, even when stretched to a breaking point. I find endless truth in this. I was definitely stretched further than I could ever imagine. Some days I just knew I would break, but by faith I was always restored and kept on going. Perseverance. Oh, how I love that word.

Chapter 34

The Joy of the Lord Is My Strength

Over the course of the past few years, many people have commented on my strength. But I assure you, it's honestly not *my* strength. Nehemiah 8:10 says, "Do not grieve, for the joy of the Lord is your strength." So simply stated, yet it says everything.

The Lord has blessed me beyond measure, and He has most definitely blessed me with joy and strength. Blessings aren't always easy or painless or expected. Anything that makes us turn to God can be a blessing, and He always comes through for us; it just may not be the way we wanted or expected. Even on the bad days, if I will only look around, there are always things that I am grateful for that bring me joy. Many things can bring us down and challenge us and our faith, but there are twice as many things to be thankful for if you just stop and think about it. Everyone's journey is different. We all have our crosses to bear, and no one can say or determine that some are heavier than others. But we are never alone!

Writing about perseverance as well as Nehemiah 8:10 reminds me of the journey of a very dear friend of mine. I knew Lisa in high school, as we occasionally played sports against one another. Although I did not know her well then, something that always stood out about her was her ability to encourage her teammates, her amazing smile, and her ability to laugh, even while on the volleyball or basketball court.

It was no coincidence that we happened to be placed on the same floor in the dorms our first year of college. God placed this amazing woman in my life for a reason. We grew to be great friends and in fact during our college years would often refer to ourselves as "the Lisa and Lisa Connection." The absolute cheesiness of that makes me laugh, but that is who we were, and we did indeed have a special connection.

We were bridesmaids in each other's weddings, and in fact certain events of her wedding are what actually tie Nehemiah 8:10 to my story. During the wedding march, her grandma collapsed in cardiac arrest. Instinctively, due to our medical background, Lisa's sister-in-law and I immediately started CPR and essentially saved her grandma's life. Once she had recuperated and was home, she sent me a plaque in the mail as a thank-you. The plaque says, "The Joy of the Lord is your Strength." To this day, I display that plaque in my dining room, as it holds so much sentimental meaning to me. Lisa and I truly had one of those friendships that no matter how long it had been since we had seen or spoken to each other we always picked right back up where we'd left off. Distance may have separated us at times, but our friendship always stayed strong. I will never forget the day I received a message from a friend who was also her cousin asking for prayers, as she was about to go into surgery. I was shocked and distraught to hear that she had been diagnosed with a brain tumor.

This cannot be possible, I thought. Lisa was the epitome of healthy. As long as I had known her she had been very health-conscious, eaten right, and exercised faithfully. Not only that, she was such a wonderful person, strong in her faith, and had already endured a lot. She and her husband battled infertility for years. They finally made the decision to adopt, and God had placed two perfectly timed opportunities in their lives and blessed them with a daughter and a son. And now they were faced with this. Ugh. I couldn't believe it was happening. *Lord, why?* was all I could think.

Lisa fought that battle with every fiber of her being. Eventually she won, but not in the way you might think. Yes, the cancer took her from this earth. But the impact that she made on hundreds of lives, and the knowledge that she was pain and cancer free and with her Lord and Savior became a great comfort. The impact that she had on me is something I will never forget and often still reflect on.

I was blessed to be able to spend some time with her during a couple of her chemotherapy appointments. I had not seen her since her diagnosis, and in fact, I can't even remember the last time I had seen her before that. I had been worried about her and completely distraught over the whole situation. But after the first time I visited with her, I had a calming peace. For the most part, looking past the physical changes that had taken place in her, she was still the same ol' Lisa to me, and that was wonderful to see. She was open and honest with me as well, which was welcome, as I had been wondering what her outlook on all this was.

It did break my heart to see her going through the horrible journey, and I remember feeling how unfair it was. It raised many questions that we will never have the answers to, and that is difficult. But she was a fighter and a huge inspiration to me and to many others. I loved her deeply, and even though we had not seen each other often over the years, we truly had that friendship that picked right up where it left off. I could have sat with her all day long. Her smile, her laugh, and her sense of humor were some of her best qualities, and it was wonderful to see those that day. I know how worried she was about many things. I wish there had been something I could do to take that worry away from her, but that was just her kind, servant heart.

In April 2015, just three months before Lisa received her angel wings, I spoke at a Christian women's conference here in Hays. It was the first time I publicly shared my story and testimony. I thought of Lisa constantly while I was writing my story, especially in many of the scriptures I shared and used for inspiration. Nehemiah 8:10 has definitely guided me in my journey. Since Jason died and after everything I went through, people have often commented to me on my strength and one day it was as if the Lord shouted this scripture at me and I realized that it truly is not my strength. It is all the Joy that the Lord has given me that gives me strength. I even titled my speech "The Joy of the Lord Is My Strength."

I know that this is where Lisa drew her strength also. I know that despite all the horrible things that happened, she was the type of person who looked at her husband, kids, and family; found abundant joy in them; and in turn drew strength. We both commented that we do not know how people without faith face these obstacles, and I am glad that we don't have to know what that is like. After visiting with her at that appointment, from some of what she shared with me, I could see the Lord at work in her and through her in many ways; maybe that is why I felt such a peace. She shared with me that she had seen Jesus and her grandparents twice in dreams, and I know that there is a reason God gave her those visions.

At another appointment we talked about the reality that she was not going to beat this. This was a hard conversation, as she talked about her husband and the kids. She kept going on and on about how wonderful her husband had been and that he had definitely "earned his ticket to heaven" through everything he had done to take care of her. She talked about their daughter and how sad she was that she would not be there for her, but she was thankful for her older sister and knew that she would be there for her for all the "girl" talks and things that moms do.

We talked a little about how resilient and matter-of-fact kids are and how wonderful it would be if we could all have childlike faith. We also talked about how my kids all handled everything, and I think that gave her some hope and comfort for her kids. The final thing I remember her telling me is how much she loved shoes. I did not remember that about her. As she was telling me that, I kept thinking about my favorite coffee cup that a friend had given me once that said, "Walk by Faith" and was covered in shoes. After that visit, I actually ordered her the same coffee cup, but then I never got a chance to give it to her.

During her year and a half battle there were many people praying for her, and she shared that she felt those prayers and was thankful for them. Her sister had started a Facebook page entitled "Run with Lisa." The page served as a place to provide friends with updates on her journey as well as provide Lisa with encouragement. Although extremely sad at times, through Lisa's journey, I gained not only inspiration but also a new perspective on the subject of miracles. In the beginning of her journey, I read a number of posts by her friends and family who would comment that they were praying for a miracle—that she would be cured of her cancer. And maybe through the course of her treatment that year and a half following her diagnosis, they did feel hopeful that she would be cured.

I know following that first surgery they were hopeful, as the doctor had felt that he was able to remove the entire tumor. But it grew back as well as spread. Lisa never gave up. She held tight to her faith as well as her family and her friends, the things that brought her joy in life. She learned not to take things for granted as she began to lose the use of her arms and legs, the same legs that carried her through many, many runs and races. "Let us run with endurance the race marked out for us, fixing our eyes on Jesus" from Hebrews 12:1–2 was the verse she held tight to. And in the end, that is exactly what she did. She fixed her eyes on Jesus. And when those who knew her best could see that she was not going to receive the "miracle" of Jesus healing her earthly body, their prayers turned to asking for the miracle of receiving eternal life with her Lord and Savior.

Near the beginning of this story I mentioned my dislike of funerals, but Lisa's service was probably the most uplifting, inspiring, comforting funeral I have attended. Yes, there were tears of sadness for sure, but there were also tears of joy knowing that my sweet, sweet friend was with Jesus and in pain no more. I felt Lisa's presence during the service and was especially touched when the priest referenced 2Corinthians 5:7, "Walk by faith, not by sight," only he personalized it for Lisa as "Run by faith." And that was the miracle. Lisa ran by faith, with endurance (also referred to as perseverance), the race that was marked out for her, fixing her eyes on Jesus. There was no doubt in my mind that she was safe in His arms.

Chapter 35

The JOurneY between Us

Second Corinthians 1:3–4 says, "Praise be to the God and Father of our Lord Jesus Christ, the Father of compassion and the God of all comfort, who comforts us in all our troubles, so that we can comfort those in any trouble with the comfort we ourselves receive from God." I once read that God allows suffering so that we might have the capacity to enter into another's sorrow and affliction, to empathize and to understand. God wants us to help each other and pay it forward. I have learned through this journey that no two situations are ever the same and you can't ever know exactly how someone feels, but I do believe that you can appreciate what they are going through, and as this scripture says, you can be there to comfort them and encourage them and give them hope, as an example of someone who has been comforted by God.

I want to touch on a book I read about joy and gratitude that changed my life. It's called *One Thousand Gifts*, by Ann Voskamp. Ann encourages us to find joy in everything, insisting that no matter what, there is always, always something to be grateful for and something to bring us joy. She teaches about the importance of journaling, writing down your thoughts, worries, and prayers, as well as keeping a gratitude journal where you simply jot down everything you encounter during your day that brings you joy.

It's a given that your faith, your family, your kids, and your friends all bring you joy, but what Ann teaches is that giving thanks for the little things around you opens your eyes and heightens your awareness of all God's blessings, not just the big, obvious ones. Her book is titled *One Thousand Gifts* because she started her gratitude journal with the goal to list a thousand things she was grateful for that brought her joy. She did indeed make it to a thousand, but then she found that she could not stop because the mere act of journaling had such a positive impact on her life.

I have to tell you one comical example of something that happened to me one day after I had read *One Thousand Gifts*. Being a stay-at-home mom becomes a tedious, thankless, routine job, and I sometimes think it's hard to find little things to be grateful for. One task in particular that never ends with a family of seven is laundry. I had been reading some of Ann's blog entries, but despite that, I was still grumbling about laundry as I went downstairs to change the loads. I was thinking to myself, *Ugh, there is nothing about laundry that really brings me joy.*

Then as I opened the dryer and pulled out the lint trap to remove the nasty lint, it was as if God slapped me on the face. I had just done a load of my girls' laundry, and the lint from that load was a shade of pink and filled with sparkles. And there was the joy. I remember immediately messaging a friend and telling her this story and how sparkly pink dryer lint brought me joy in doing laundry. We thought that "Sparkly Dryer Lint" would be a great title for a blog someday.

I love Facebook. I do. I know a lot of people don't care for it or get tired of all the negativity and other nonsense that often surfaces. And yes, there is definitely an overabundance of it. But I just don't allow myself to get wrapped up in any of that. I use it to keep in touch with friends, see pictures of their kids, and find out what weekly specials are out there in restaurant land or what the cupcake of the day is at the local bakery. I also follow many Christian-based pages, authors, public figures, etc. I truly draw a lot of daily inspiration and encouragement from these pages and people. I often use it as a platform to share my thoughts and feelings in hopes of encouraging others by my faith and testimony. As I conclude this book, this excerpt of my journey, I want to share this quote and Facebook post from Proverbs 31 Ministries from November 19, 2013 because I think it perfectly summarizes so many points I have pondered in this story.

"We must choose to trust the Plan Maker even though our faith is small, and we cannot understand the plan." —Mary Southerland

Here on earth we all have many questions, many "Why?"s. We can drive ourselves crazy pondering all these questions and whys, making life even more difficult. They truly *do not* make a whole lot of sense a lot of the time, but by building and constantly growing our faith, we *can* learn to trust in God's plan and let the Holy Spirit fill our hearts and allow acceptance. This is not always immediate; it can take time, and that is OK. Life is about choices, and as Mary Sutherland said, we must "choose to trust." We can choose to be angry or bitter, but doesn't that make life even harder? We will all have our down days, but the good days will certainly outshine the bad when we choose to lean on our faith to guide us and focus on our blessings. We are never alone. Not only is God with us always, but He places people in our lives for a reason: to love us, support us, cry with us, laugh with us, help us grow and heal, and accompany us on our journeys. We are far more blessed than we are burdened; we just must choose to look at it this way. Choose to find the joy in each day, and allow gratitude to fill your hearts and minds.

I am not an expert by any means, but I have learned a lot through the trials and experiences I have been through, especially in the past ten years. I can't speak for anyone but myself because everyone's journey is different, but if my testimony can inspire and help just one person, then I am thankful that the Lord is at work through me.

This year (2018) will mark the ten-year "angel anniversary" for our family. Jason and Cari flew to be with the angels almost ten years ago. What I imagine to be a glorious journey for them left an earthly family with way too many unanswered questions and sadness. I cannot keep the tears from flowing as I write this, reflect back ten years ago, and then look at today. Two widowed, heartbroken young people became acquainted as a result of tragedy. They became an instant support system for one another, truly saving each other's lives. Neither one expected to fall in love so soon; in fact, neither one thought they could find love again. Both were devastated thinking that their children would have to grow up with only one parent. But this was not to be; it was not God's plan. I have no other explanation for this journey other than divine intervention.

Our lives may not always be easy today, but our blessings far outweigh our burdens, and I have to praise and thank *God* constantly for bringing our families together. And to bind us even tighter, a new child blessed our lives. Does this not all show *God* at work? It's all still amazing to me. As far as I am concerned, I have allowed many of my question marks to turn to exclamation marks. That's what faith can do.

I leave you with this final reflection. Remember that no matter what you may be going through, (1) you are not alone; whether thanks to the people the Lord places in our lives or the presence of the Lord Himself, we are never alone. (2) We are overcomers simply because Jesus was an overcomer, and there is nothing we cannot overcome with Him on our side. And finally, (3) we are far more blessed than we are burdened, and we must choose to look at it this way. Choose to find the JOY in each day and in your JOurneY, allow gratitude to fill your hearts and your minds, and let the joy of the Lord be your strength.

Acknowledgments

I feel incredibly blessed that what started as a simple journal to record my thoughts and these events of my life became a platform to share my faith walk in hopes of inspiring and encouraging others.

I truly give all the glory to my Lord and Savior for not only placing the idea to share my journey on my heart but for shaping, molding, and guiding me along this faith walk and orchestrating the events of my life that have led to my testimony. I truly believe the Lord and His angels watch over and walk beside us each and every day, and on the days when we are unable to walk ourselves, they carry us.

Countless family members, friends, and acquaintances have encouraged me to write this book, and I am very thankful for your kind words and support. It has truly given me the courage and motivation to pursue this adventure. I want to especially thank my GAB, Heal Your Heart, and Vibrant Happy Women ladies. Your fellowship, friendship, love, prayers, and support mean more to me than I can even express.

I want to extend a special thank-you to Tammy Lee Schumacher, intuitive soul healer and international best-selling author of *The Second Start, Finding JOY in the New You,* for sharing your knowledge and experience in writing and publishing your book. I also want to thank Erin Lyn Burks, author of *Twice the Blessing* and *Every Day Is a Gift,* not only for sharing your expertise in writing and self-publishing but for giving me insight, feedback, and support in writing mine as well. I am also so very thankful for everyone at WestBow Press who contributed to this project and for helping me become a published author.

To all the named and unnamed characters in this story, I can't thank you enough for being a part of my life and for allowing me to mention your role in my journey. God truly places people in our lives for a reason.

Even though faith is a personal walk, many people have contributed to helping me grow in my faith. Aside from my parents, family, and church families, I hold a very special place in my heart for Pastor Dennis Carter and his wife, Betty; Pastor Becky Saddler, Pastor Berniece Ludlum, and Reverend Delbert Stanton. God truly spoke to me through the words and actions of all of you amazing people during the time frame of this story.

I don't know many people who have three amazing sets of in-laws, but we sure do. Joe and Lynette Kanak were my first in-laws, and I am blessed and thankful to be a part of the Kanak family. That Jason was such a wonderful, kind, caring man is a reflection of you and the rest of your family. Ed and Carolyn Winebrenner, you welcomed and accepted me from day one. To lose a child has got to be the most heart-wrenching experience, but these two families have shown us boundless love and support, and I hope you all know how much we appreciate that, as well as everything you have done and do for us. Harry and Barbara McGrath, you also welcomed me and my children into your family with open arms. I know losing your daughter-in-law and watching your son experience that heartache was difficult, but you also lovingly supported us in our relationship without reservation. We truly cannot thank our parents and in-laws enough for the unending support and love they have shown and continue to show us. They are all phenomenal grandparents as well, and our children are privileged to have them all in their lives.

I never had sisters growing up, so I was thrilled to inherit sisters by marriage. Linda, you were my first sister-in-law, and you definitely had a key role in the events of this story. If I've never officially thanked you for "introducing" me to Scott, well, here is your thank-you! Your love and support despite your own grief have been selfless and appreciated more than you could ever know. You, Ryan, and the kids are special to me, and I love you very much!

I am also very thankful that I inherited two more sisters (and three more brothers) by marrying Scott. Melissa and Sean, I will never forget the first time we met as well as our Florida trip and how welcoming you both were to me. Amy, you and I have a lot in common, especially being married to McGrath brothers, and you and Dave were also so kind and supportive. Erick, you are a gentle giant with a huge heart! I know losing your sister left a void in your life that could never be filled, but I am so glad that you have allowed me to be a sister to you. Besides, I like claiming you as my brother so that I can say I am related to a famous drummer. I have no doubt that Cari is looking down on you, a very proud big sister smiling with that beautiful signature smile of hers.

Next to being a mom, being an aunt is pretty amazing, so kudos to all of you for blessing me with that wonderful opportunity! Tessa, Cy, Evan, Parker, Grady, Danni, Thomas, Daeton, and Carissa, I know there is a part of all of us that wishes you could have known your Uncle Jason or Aunt Cari, but Scott and I could not be happier to be your uncle and aunt! We love you all beyond words!

I have the most amazing family in the entire world. My mom, Diana, and my dad, Richard, have always been my biggest fans. I truly have no way to express my deep gratitude to you both for everything you have done and continue to do for me and our family. As mentioned over and over in these pages, Mom, you are my rock, and I thank God every day for giving me the best, most supportive mom ever. Along with my parents I want to thank my brothers and their wives, Todd and Amanda and Brett and Leah and my adorable nephew Jackson and niece Adaline as well as my late grandparents, Karl and Mary Belle Jennison and Walter and Etta Fern Ashcraft, and all my aunts, uncles, and cousins for everything you all have done to show your love and support over the years. Family is *everything* to me, and I was blessed with the best for sure!

To my kids, Benton, Jaren, Lilian, Lynsi, and Layci, you are my world. Becoming a mom was one of the most amazing, exciting, fulfilling experiences of my life. Before I even became a mom, I thought I wanted four kids. Little did I know I would go from the mom of one to the mom of four in such a short time. And then to add one more to the fabulousness that is now the Fab Five—well, what can I say? It just works and was clearly meant to be. You are all very special gifts from God, and I can only hope and pray that you all know how much you are loved and adored and how very proud I am to be your mom. Each one of you holds a very special and unique place in my heart and even though I did not give birth to you, Benton and Lilian, you are my son and daughter, and I am so thankful that you accepted me and love me as your mom. I pray that despite the tragedy of losing a parent, you four older kids will feel that God brought us all together as a family and that you will always appreciate and lean on your faith in whatever you are faced with in this life. Always remember: "You can do all things through Christ who strengthens you." I love you all so much.

Scott, because of you, I laugh, I smile, and I dare to dream again. I look forward with great joy to spending the rest of my life with you, caring for you, nurturing you, and being there for you in all life has in store for us, and I vow to be true and faithful for as long as we both shall live. I loved these vows when we chose them, and I love them even more as I read them today. Thank you for always being right beside me on this journey. Your love and support means the world to me. Thank you for allowing and encouraging me to share our journey. I am proud and honored to be your wife. I love you!

Last but certainly not least, I want to honor the memory of Cari and Jason, our amazing guardian angels. This year (2018) it will be ten years since you both flew to be with the Lord and His heavenly angels. Your departures from this earth left heartache and many unanswered questions, but by faith, God granted us healing, comfort, and peace in knowing that you are safe in His loving arms and watching over us all. I am often reminded of your presence when I look at the pink and orange and blue colors of the sky at sunset, knowing that they were your favorite colors. We also think of you when we look into the eyes of the children or when they make a familiar facial expression or gesture that reminds us of you. Your legacies both live on through them for sure. You both touched countless lives and continue to do so through all the wonderful, cherished memories.

About the Author

Lisa grew up in the small western Kansas town of Healy, where she was active in everything imaginable in school, church, and her community. She graduated from high school in 1996 and attended Fort Hays State University where she received a B.S. degree in medical diagnostic imaging.

Lisa is married to Scott, and they have five children: Benton, Jaren, Lilian, Lynsi, and Layci. They live in Hays, Kansas, where aside from schedule juggling for five busy children, Lisa also works PRN as a mammographer. The family attends the First United Methodist Church where Lisa leads a women's Bible study group, GAB (Girlfriends and the Bible).

Lisa is very passionate about her faith as well as sharing her story in hopes of inspiring and encouraging others in their faith walk. On numerous occasions people have commented that she is a very strong person to have endured what she and her family have and to be where they are today. To this she replies: "Nehemiah 8:10 says it best, 'The joy of the Lord is my strength.'"

CPSIA information can be obtained
at www.ICGtesting.com
Printed in the USA
LVHW111213300921
699074LV00001B/3